An Hour of American History

An Hour of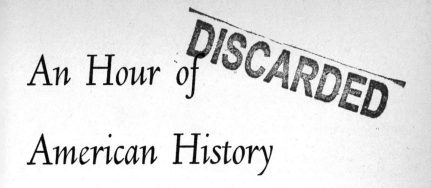

American History

From Columbus to Coolidge

by Samuel Eliot Morison

REVISED EDITION

"The office of America is to liberate."—Emerson

BEACON PRESS   BOSTON

Foreword

This little book was written during the Coolidge administration and published in 1929. Its original title, *An Hour of American History*, meant that it could be read through in one hour.

In this new edition I have not attempted to extend the story to cover the tremendous events of the last thirty years but have only indicated, toward the close, that both readers and myself are well aware of them. In general, my long if foreshortened view of American history has not been changed; and my final paragraph of hope and confidence in America's destiny has weathered the depression and the cold war.

S. E. Morison

BOSTON, MASSACHUSETTS
DECEMBER 1959

Contents

CHAPTER ONE

Foundation to 1760

During the hundreds of thousands of years when Europe and Asia were growing out of savagery into what we call civilization, the American continent remained as separate as if it had been another planet.

Something more than twenty-five thousand and less than fifty thousand years ago, the ancestors of the people we call the American Indians crossed over from Asia into a probably uninhabited continent. It must have taken them many, many years, or even centuries, to make the passage by the Bering Strait. All intercourse between the Eastern and the Western Hemispheres then ceased, except that the Eskimos passed back and forth in the Arctic but never pressed far south. The Polynesians, marvelous navigators that they were in their outrigger canoes, never settled nearer America than Easter Island, 2,000 miles off the coast of Chile. The people of Europe and Africa were less venturesome, and if an occasional Chinese junk was blown across the Pacific, there is no record of it in Indian art, culture, or folklore.

Other Asiatic tribes migrated westward and settled in Europe and northern Africa. The dynasties of Babylon, Chaldea, and Egypt rose and fell. Aristotle proved that the earth was round like a ball; Eratosthenes said that you could sail from Europe due west to India; and Seneca foretold that one day a new world would be discovered in the mysterious ocean that lay between the western shores of Europe and the eastern shores of Asia. But no one, so far as we know, made the attempt; and in the dark ages that followed, only scholars believed that it was possible. Even in China, the land of long memories, all record or tradition of a transpacific kindred vanished.

About one thousand years after the birth of Christ, a Norseman named Eric the Red lifted a corner of the veil, without knowing it. He discovered and colonized Greenland. His son Leif, blown before an easterly gale in his trading ship, blundered upon a coast where wild grapes grew, and a few years later some of his kindred wintered there. The story was treasured in Icelandic folklore, but it suggested nothing to Europeans just emerging from barbarism. Three centuries later, Europe resumed the quest for a sea route to India, but the isolation of America endured until Columbus had the courage to sail westward, on and on.

During the long, long time that had elapsed since their passage from Asia, the Indians spread widely over North, Central, and South America. Hundreds of physical types and dialects were developed, as different one from another as were the races and languages of western Europe. In New Mexico there are ruins of cities older than Troy and Cnossus. The Mayan calendar, justly characterized by Tozzer as "the most remarkable achievement of the intellect in the new world," began to function in 613 B.C.

First in Guatemala and then in Yucatan, the Mayas built those amazing temples, palaces, and monuments that are the most original artistic achievements on this continent. Then, just as the Romans conquered the Greeks and absorbed their culture, so, about the year 1200 of our era, the Toltecs, led by a great scholar-priest and warrior-king named Quetzalcoatl, conquered the Mayan nation and accepted its civilization. Within two centuries the Toltec empire was destroyed by the Aztecs, wild hunters from the north, who in turn were taught by their conquerors.

Another century elapsed. The Aztec empire and the Inca kingdom in Peru enjoyed that comfortable stability which is the goal of cautious statesmanship. In the northern forests the virile Iroquois showed some promise of political genius, and more than a threat of westward expansion. Yet so feeble were the Indians' weapons of offense (for they knew not the use of iron), so primitive their methods of transportation (for they never discovered the wheel or built a boat), and so plenteous the food supply that centuries more might have elapsed without disturbing the balance of power, unless an outside element broke into the red man's continent.

All hope of an enduring peace vanished on October 12, 1492, when the fleet of Christopher Columbus dropped anchor off Guanahani (which he named San Salvador), an island outpost of the Arawaks. These simple natives believed that gods, or men like gods, had come to them in the white caravels with purple sails; they soon learned better. Columbus believed that Japan and China lay just over the horizon; even his later voyages failed to convince this man of ardent faith and dogged persistence that he had discovered a completely new world. Yet a new era in the world's history had begun. Columbus' discovery meant for the natives, whom he insisted on naming Indians, the choice between slavery, absorption, or extermination. For men of Columbus' color and race, it meant a fresh outlet for energies then rapidly expanding, a new source of wealth, refuge for the discontented, hope for the dispossessed—and many other things still beyond our ken.

Although a Genoese by birth, Columbus sailed under authority of the Spanish sovereigns. On later voyages he founded the first Spanish colony and discovered the mainland; but the continent was named America after Amerigo Vespucci, an Italian pilot who knew how to advertise himself. John Cabot, a Venetian resident in England, discovered Newfoundland or Nova Scotia in 1497, but over a century elapsed before England was ready to colonize. A Breton mariner, Jacques Cartier, discovered the Gulf of St. Lawrence in 1533, but not until 1608 did Champlain plant the lilies of France on the rock of Quebec. Pedro Cabral, sailing a Portuguese fleet to India, happened upon Brazil in 1500, and that region was awarded to Portugal by the Pope.

Broadly speaking, the sixteenth century in America was the century of Spain. Alone of the European states she had achieved unity and internal peace, thus releasing for overseas adventure pioneers and conquerors like Balboa, who discovered the Pacific Ocean; Cortez, the conqueror of Mexico; Pizarro, who seized the Inca empire in Peru; Ponce de Leon, who settled Puerto Rico and discovered Florida; Coronado, who marched with men in armor as far north as Kansas; de Soto, who discovered the Mississippi; and Orellana, who crossed the Andes from the west and sailed down the Amazon to its mouth. Others, priests and laymen, transplanted European civilization to North and South America. No other nation dared challenge the supremacy of Spain, and the wealth she drew from the New World almost enabled her to lay the Old World at her feet.

Wealth has been the primary object of all colonization in modern times. The means of obtaining it—as determined by climate, transportation, natural resources, and the character of the natives—have shaped the varied forms that modern colonization has assumed. In Africa and the Far East, where the climate was unsuitable for white settlement and the natives were ready to trade, it was sufficient for the European purpose to establish trading posts and forts. In America the combination of unattractive climate and trading natives existed only in the far north, where French Canada until 1760, and the Hudson's Bay establishments until the present, were a mere chain of fur-trading posts. The

Spaniards, on the contrary, reached regions of great natural wealth, inhabited by non-trading peoples. They had to exploit and administer—in other words, to colonize—in order to get out something more than the Indians' superfluous ornaments.

Climatic conditions throughout the greater part of Spanish America were such that a European could not support himself by tilling the soil. The newcomers therefore attempted to work the natives. In Brazil the Indians escaped to the jungle; in the West Indies they resisted and were exterminated. Negro slaves, accordingly, were imported from Africa. Elsewhere the Indians were tractable, and in Mexico and Peru the Spaniards had only to replace a native ruling class in order to have a vast labor force ready to do their bidding on plantation, mine, and ranch. Hence Spanish America became an empire of servile or semi-servile labor—exploited, administered, and converted to Christianity by a white aristocracy. Every colonizing power in America made sincere efforts to protect the Indians from cruelty and injustice, but all except France were thwarted by the attitude of white pioneers toward men of color. If the Anglo-American frontiersman acted upon the maxim, "A good Indian is a dead Indian," it was because he was unable to persuade the red man, as the Spaniard had done, to be a working man.

The Spanish view of colonies as producers of raw materials for home supply, and markets for home manufactures, was shared by almost every European statesman until the mid-nineteenth century and accepted by all European colonists until 1775. To enforce these views, the Spanish government created a system of colonial administration that was the envy of other powers. Spanish America was allowed to trade only with Spain, and only through the port of Seville. The colonists were not allowed to export—or, in some instances, even to produce—articles that would compete with Spanish products. These laws, with others regulating in minute detail the affairs of colonists and natives, were made in Spain by a royal council and enforced through officials appointed by the king. It was a despotism tempered by graft and smuggling; but Spaniards at home had nothing better, and Spaniards in the colonies wanted nothing different. The republican principle came to Spanish America in the nineteenth century by way of imitation—not, as in English America, by slow growth from within.

The heroic age of Spanish discovery and colonization reached its acme in 1580, when Philip II added the Portuguese empire to his own vast domains. The first milestone in the heroic age of English discovery was passed the same year, when Francis Drake, returning home from around the world with the spoil of Spanish treasure galleons, was knighted on the deck of his flagship by Queen Elizabeth.

England was not ready to expand overseas until after James I had concluded peace with Spain in 1604. During the next thirty-five years, English island colonies (such as Antigua, Bermuda, and Barbados) and the continental colonies of Virginia, Maryland, and New England were founded. We must not think of the continental colonies at that time as identical with the present states of the same name. They were, rather, feeble settlements clinging to the seacoast and the navigable rivers, threatened by the Indians and not beyond the reach of famine, numbering in 1640 less than 30,000 white people. Measured by what Spain had done a century before, these settlements were as poor in wealth as in renown; yet in them the English principles and institutions through which the United States is still governed had already taken root.

Spanish colonization since Columbus' first experiment had been largely a matter of government enterprise. The

Crown selected the colonists (carefully excluding Jews and heretics), paid their passage, and governed them after they arrived. England wanted colonies for no higher purpose than Spain, but the English Crown was too poor to finance colonization and too weak to control it. Hence the English settlements were founded by individuals and corporate groups; these differed much from each other in quality and purpose, yet all managed to obtain privileges that exempted them in great measure from government control.

Virginia, the first English colony, was founded by the favorite English method, as a joint-stock corporation. "Adventurers"—that is, stockholders who ventured their money for mixed motives of patriotism and profit—subscribed to the Virginia Company, which received from the Crown a charter granting it the land, trade, and government between certain parallels of latitude from sea to sea.

Owing to inexperience, Jamestown (1607) passed through the same vicissitudes as the first colony of Columbus in 1493 and many others in the sixteenth century. An ill-chosen ship's company, composed of about equal parts of jailbirds and gentlemen volunteers, weak and dizzy after a long voyage in a crowded, unsanitary ship, settled on a culture-bed of malaria. High hopes of finding gold and spices were quickly dissipated. The Indians, at first friendly and inquisitive, became offish and hostile when the white men stole their corn and tampered with their women. Famine and fever brought scenes too dreadful to relate. The survivors were saved only through the iron discipline of a few leaders: Captain John Smith, Sir Thomas Dale, and Sir Thomas Gates. But even with their pluck and persistence, only 150 colonists were left at Jamestown in 1610 out of the 900 who had landed there since 1607. Yet they did not give up hope, and from one of the survivors came these brave words:

Be not dismayed at all
For scandall cannot doe us wrong,
    God will not let us fall.
Let England knowe our willingnesse,
    For that our worke is good;
Wee hope to plant a nation
    Where none before hath stood.

However gallant the spirit of the Virginia planters, there was a limit to the good money that English stockholders were willing to throw after the bad. That limit had almost been reached in 1616, when John Rolfe, the husband of Pocahontas, discovered a way of growing and curing the wild Virginia tobacco so that it could be smoked with more pleasure to the senses than pain to the tongue. The government gave it a monopoly of the English market; and the Virginia Company, in order to encourage settlement, granted fifty acres of land to every immigrant or to the colonist who paid for the immigrant's passage. In 1619, as an additional inducement, the first legislature in the New World was granted to Virginia. By these measures the colony was saved and became a success. With the proceeds of his first tobacco crop, a Virginian could buy the services of an English laborer for five years and, by paying his passage over, increase his holding of land. With ordinary luck and diligence, he could become in a few years' time a considerable planter, perhaps one of the "First Families of Virginia."

Settlement was greatly dispersed, owing to the desire of each planter to have a water frontage on a river or bay and plenty of room for expansion inland. Few schools were established; churches were difficult to keep up; and there was little community life. Hence Virginia became the original home of American individualism; instead of levelling down social distinctions, Virginia created them. Vast estates gave the successful shopkeeper a landed-gentry outlook on life. Overproduction of tobacco and a long period of low prices squeezed out the small producers in favor of the bigger planters, who had the credit to obtain Negroes from the slave traders and the wit to go in for mass production.

In spite of the growth of aristocracy, or perhaps because of it, the political life of Virginia remained healthy and vigorous. James I dissolved the Company in 1624, but did not molest the political privileges of the colonists; they continued to elect the lower house of their legislature, which, with an executive council appointed by the royal governor, granted lands, laid out roads, organized courts of justice and a militia force, established the Church of England, passed a criminal code, and inspected tobacco. The planters came to regard their political and social privileges as absolute rights; and Virginia produced a race of leaders who first created, then almost destroyed, the United States.

Maryland, another tobacco colony, was granted by the Crown to George Calvert, Lord Baltimore, as a feudal estate. The Lord Proprietor had full control over both land and government, with the interesting exception that his laws must have the consent of the freemen—and Englishmen refused to give their consent in any other way than by the vote of an elected legislature. Lord Baltimore, a Roman Catholic, probably intended his colony to be a refuge for Englishmen of that faith, but he sold land to Anglicans as well. He had a difficult course to steer, between jealous Protestants in England and zealous Jesuits in Maryland. In order to retain his property and keep the peace, an early legislature passed at his bidding a Toleration Act (1649), which was repealed by the Protestants as soon as they had the power.

The voyage of the famous *Mayflower* (1620), bringing an even hundred Pilgrims to New Plymouth, established the first of the New England colonies. Strip their history of the false sentiment overlaid by romancers; get down to the bed-rock of Governor Bradford's annals; and you have an inspiring story of faith and courage, a microcosm of the great experiment that is America. For those Pilgrims were a kindly, simple group of English Puritans, with all the idealism and integrity of that way of life. In a material way they did little more than demonstrate that by faith and character (with some aid from corn, the beaver, and the humble clam) human life could be sustained on the New England coast. Spiritually their contribution was incalculable.

Massachusetts Bay was the real mother colony of New England. John Winthrop, Thomas Dudley, and a few score Puritan gentry, pinched by the rising cost of living and unable to impose their views on the Church of England, aimed at no less a goal than to transplant English civilization, purged of its corruption; to found in America an English commonwealth based on the word of God, as revealed in the Bible and interpreted by themselves. Obtaining control of a colonizing corporation called the Massachusetts Bay Company, this Puritan group did not attempt, like the founders of Virginia, to govern colonists from London. Rather, it transferred both corporation and settlers to Boston (1630), where, after a few years of struggle and adjustment, the charter became an efficient constitution of government.

This corporate form of government was not necessarily democratic. In Massachusetts the franchise was given only to communicants of the Puritan churches. But the election of both executive and legislature by the same voters and at fixed dates made the colony even less dependent on England than was Virginia, whose royal governor enjoyed considerable power and patronage. The corporate form became so popular with English colonists that it set the standard for state government in the Revolution, and the present political system of the United States is more nearly derived from it than from any other source.

As the Puritans emigrated largely in neighborhood groups, they also settled in communities and established the famous town meetings, which gave every settler at least a voice in local affairs. Until settlement became more dense, each man had also a free house and tillage lot, with a share in the common pastures and meadows. In these village groups —the New England towns—can be found the germ of American community spirit and neighborliness, with their defects of intolerance and snooping; as in the Virginia plantation, we find the germ of American individualism, with its defects of occasional lawlessness and violence.

King Charles I and Bishop Laud were making England so unpleasant for Puritans in the 1630's that in ten years about fifteen thousand of them came to Massachusetts Bay. There they proceeded to make things difficult for one another. Winthrop, Dudley, Endecot, and the Puritan clergy believed they had a divine commission to maintain a particular faith called Calvinism, a particular form of church government called Congregationalism, and a strict code of personal morality. Many of the colonists had other views and were no more gentle in expressing them than the Massachusetts government was in suppressing them. It seemed monstrous to the colonists that the persecuted should turn persecutors, and unreasonable to those in power that their beliefs should be challenged in the very narrow strip of territory allotted to the Massachusetts Bay Company.

Roger Williams, a charming and earnest young preacher, declared the Massachusetts churches to be "ulcered and gangrened." For this and other offenses he was banished. So were the followers of Ann Hutchinson, who set the whole colony in an uproar by claiming special revelations unflattering to the clergy. For these and other dissenters, Williams founded the colony of Rhode Island on the basis of civil and religious liberty (1636). There every man was free to worship God as he chose, or not at all, and no man was compelled to support a church to which he did not belong. No such complete separation of church and state had then been adopted in any Christian country; few have gone so far even today. We can hardly rate Roger Williams too high among the standard bearers of liberty.

Connecticut, the fourth New England colony, was also settled out of Massachusetts Bay, but by orthodox Puritans who gave no better reason than the strong bent of their spirits to remove thither. It was the fertile soil of the Connecticut Valley that induced this first of the countless westward migrations—a movement that carried Englishmen and then Americans every year a little nearer the setting sun.

The founders of New England, like all emigrants to America, hoped for prosperity but seem to have had no clear idea how to get it. The soil afforded a bare subsistence but no staple of ready sale in England, such as Virginia tobacco, and the Indians had little fur to sell. For the New Englanders, then, the problem was not how to obtain cheap labor, but how to exist. Maritime enterprise was the answer.

The West Indies, which were falling into English and French hands, proved an ideal market for the products of northern forests, farms, and waters. A score of little seaport towns from Portsmouth, New Hampshire, to New Haven, Connecticut, built their own ships and sailed them—laden with salt codfish and lumber, corn and provisions, livestock, and woodenware whittled out by farmers in the long winter evenings—to Barbados, Martinique, and Jamaica, whence they returned with molasses to make New England rum and "pieces of eight" to buy English luxuries. No wonder the cod became almost as sacred as the Book, and that English statesmen who endeavored to protect the one were suspected of trampling on the other.

These maritime developments were regarded by the Puritan leaders as a signal mark of divine favor to His poor saints in the wilderness, for Calvinism taught that the just man could serve God best in following his chosen career: that success was a mark of grace. Yet a little while and success would be god, and the advertising profession its priesthood. The Puritan faith nonetheless nurtured many spiritual seeds and tender intellectual plants in the rough wilderness where such things die. In order to teach every child to read the Bible, the New England colonies established free schools in almost every village; and in order to keep up a supply of educated ministers, Harvard College was founded in 1636. But children who learned to read the Bible began to find forbidden meanings in it; Yale had to be founded in 1701 to offset Harvard liberalism; and independent congregations might and did go over to Unitarianism. Thus Massachusetts, dedicated to one true faith, became the cradle of many faiths—and Boston, in turn, a provincial Geneva, Athens, and Rome.

Life in early New England was severe and bleak, but early discipline held down frontier lawlessness. Even those who dislike the curious blend of public spirit and private gain, independence and inhibition, reverence and self-righteousness in the Yankee character must admit that it has contributed to America's intellectual and moral life in the same degree that the Virginian character has contributed to American amenity, statesmanship, and military strategy.

Of this New England group of colonies, only New Hampshire and Massachusetts had any sort of authority from the English Crown; the rest were self-governing squatters. Charles I was about to pull them all up short when he fell into difficulties at home. Through his Civil War with the Long Parliament, all the English colonies remained practically neutral, and their connection with the mother country became even more slender than before. New England even formed its own confederation for protection against the Indians and the Dutch.

The Dutch colony of New Netherland was founded by a trading corporation in 1614, following Henry Hudson's discovery of the river that bears his name. That river drained the best fur-producing region south of Canada—the country of the Iroquois, whose friendship was secured by an alcoholic dinner on board Hudson's *Half Moon*. Since Washington Irving published his *Knickerbocker's History*, with its jolly caricatures of the Dutch governors and burghers, it has been difficult to regard New Netherland seriously; and as the colony enjoyed no self-government, it left no trace on American institutions. Albany and Manhattan (founded 1624) attracted the ships and traders of all nations; great feudal manors along the Hudson were granted to ambitious Dutchmen and Flemings. The Swedes established fur-trading posts on the Delaware River, which were absorbed by New Netherland (1655), as that colony was by the English.

Charles II, in contempt of public law but in accordance with the national instinct to expand, granted New Netherland to his brother James, Duke of York, in 1664. So disaffected from trading-company rule were the Dutch colonists that when the Duke's officials arrived at Manhattan to take possession, New Netherland became the English province of New York without a struggle.

Pennsylvania and the two Carolinas were the results of a second wave of English colonizing activity between 1660 and 1690. William Penn was a wealthy Quaker who made his colony, like Rhode Island, a refuge for oppressed Christians of whatever sect or race. Complete religious liberty, good soil, and the favorable situation of Philadelphia for commerce combined to attract English and Irish Quakers, German dissenters (the "Pennsylvania Dutch") and Scots-Irish from Ulster. These different elements did not love one another, as William Penn had hoped; but under a liberal and tolerant government, they managed to rub along together fairly well and to prosper greatly. With Penn's descendants, who regarded the colony as an income producer, their relations were unpleasant. Philadelphia became the largest town in the colonies (population 18,000 in 1760) and the most civilized, as everyone who met her leading citizen, Benjamin Franklin, was ready to admit.

New Jersey was granted to two groups of proprietors, some of them Quakers, in 1664. About the same time, Carolina—which comprised all territory between Virginia and Florida—was granted to a proprietary body whose leading spirit was Anthony Ashley Cooper, later Earl of Shaftesbury. It was soon separated into two very unlike colonies: North Carolina, a favorite home for industrious farmers from Virginia; and South Carolina, where fortunes were made from producing rice and indigo with slave labor. Charleston (founded 1680) became a southern rival to New York and Philadelphia in the following century.

Georgia, last of the thirteen colonies, was founded in 1733 by charitable Englishmen in order to give poor men a new start in life and to provide a buffer against Spanish Florida. The two goals did not mix well; but after an early prohibition of rum and slaves was lifted, Georgia became a prosperous planter colony like South Carolina.

So much for the founding of the thirteen colonies. The haphazard, individual method of establishing them made it difficult to fit them into a colonial system when, about 1660, England woke up to the fact that she had an empire. Thereafter, successive efforts were made by the English government to bring them under some sort of control, so that for-

eigners would not get the profits of their trade. The Navigation Acts of 1662-96—similar in principle to the Spanish Laws
of the Indies, though freer in practice—stopped most of the
direct trading between the English colonies and continental
Europe, while protecting colonial products and shipping
from European competition. James II abolished self-government in the northern colonies (1685), but when his throne
was usurped by William III, the Americans snapped back
into their old governments and ways.

William III and his successors left the colonies a substantial measure of home rule but gave most of them royal
governors, vetoed such laws as conflicted with one another or
with English interests, and managed to enforce the Navigation Acts at least as well as most laws were enforced in those
days. It was an illogical system, but all English government
lacks logic, and the colonies thrived under it, increasing in
population from 100,000 in 1665 to over 1,500,000 in 1760.
They spread up to the Appalachian Mountains and beat off,
with English assistance, every effort of the French and
Spaniards to conquer them. In spite of petty irritations, the
British Empire seemed in 1760 to be growing peacefully into
the commonwealth of free nations that it has finally become.
The American Revolution interrupted this process and gave
birth to the United States of America.

CHAPTER TWO

Revolution: 1760-1789

The causes of the American Revolution were many, but they all boil down to this: a parent attempted to treat lusty youths as if they were small children. The thirteen colonies in 1770 already included more people than Australia would have a century later, or than Canada could show in 1860. The backwoods from New Hampshire to Georgia were filling up with hardy pioneers who disliked all restraint and to whom the name of England evoked but dim memories of far-off, unhappy, hungry days.

A half-century of warfare, culminating in Wolfe's victory of 1759, expelled France from the New World but created fresh causes of dissension. The colonists declared they had been dragged into war by European diplomats and that England had secured the spoils; the English accused the colonists of being selfish and grasping, bawling for help when the Indians cut loose and then going home while British regulars did the fighting. There was some truth in both views, and much wrong.

In every war of the eighteenth century, the English government had been hampered by certain colonies which refused to pull their weight, traded with the enemy, and stirred up the Indians by robbing and cheating them. Accordingly, the young and energetic King George III and his mininsters planned at the world peace of 1763 to stop the leaks in the Navigation Acts, to introduce more system into colonial government, to maintain a big garrison of regulars in the colonies, to take over (as the federal government later did) all matters of Indians and public lands, and to raise part of the expense by taxing the colonists. The opening numbers of this program passed almost unnoticed, but the Stamp Act of 1765, requiring legal documents to be drawn up on paper stamped and sold by the government, was resisted so stiffly that Parliament repealed it. Other taxes were levied, and repealed in turn (1770). Yet, by reorganizing the colonial customs service, enforcing new Navigation Acts, and stamping out smuggling, the British exchequer did manage to get some revenue out of the colonies—though never enough to meet the cost of military protection.

All these experiments gave rise to energetic discussion and led the colonists to formulate their rights, which they had had slight occasion to do before. Men like James Otis, John Adams, Thomas Jefferson, and John Dickinson wrote lengthy treatises to prove that, as Englishmen, they could not be taxed by a legislature to which they did not elect representatives. English writers such as William Knox and Dr. Johnson argued that colonists were no more exempt from parliamentary taxation than were the people of Manchester, who elected no member to the House of Commons.

Colonial leaders insisted that home rule was the essence of the British political structure and that "Rights" were the foundation of liberty. Somewhat vaguely they grasped the federal principle: Parliament *might* have supreme power over such matters as waging war, making treaties, and regulating inter-imperial commerce, but the colonial legislatures *must* have complete power over their internal affairs. British liberals were willing to concede much in order to save trouble, but even they could not comprehend the federal theory. All Englishmen at home thought in terms of a central, unified government: the King in Parliament was sovereign of the whole empire, and British subjects must obey the law.

Unable to persuade the mother country to accept their

view of her constitution, the colonists had only one recourse: to get out. Americans could not possibly admit that a parliament 3000 miles away had unlimited power to legislate for them; nor have they ever allowed such power to their own elected Congress.

The immediate cause of the final rupture was only remotely connected with taxation. A mob marshaled by Samuel Adams destroyed some valuable property in the "Boston Tea Party" of 1773. This was by no means the first offense of Boston and Massachusetts against law and order. Parliament attempted to punish the town by closing its port and to discipline the colony by altering its government, but succeeded only in showing the other colonies that they must hang together or hang separately. Virginia summoned a convention of colonial delegates to Philadelphia, in Continental Congress. The compromise they offered was refused by the king, and the boycott they attempted did not work.

Fighting broke out in Massachusetts, Virginia, and North Carolina in the spring of 1775. In June the Continental Congress appointed George Washington commander in chief of the colonial forces besieging the British garrison in Boston. Having appealed to arms, it was uesless for the colonists to expect the English government to give way. George III, like most employers with a strike on their hands, wished to suppress before he would negotiate. Yet so hopeful were the colonists of a political overturn in England, so reluctant to break altogether with the mother country, that the war continued more than fifteen months before Congress declared: "That these United Colonies are, and of Right ought to be, Free and Independent States."

Such, in brief, were the immediate causes of the American Revolution. Many books have been written to explain the fundamental causes. Certain historians, not understanding why such a fuss should have been made over a few rea-

sonable taxes, have insisted that the Revolution was a nationalist movement, promoted by the propaganda of clever
politicians like Sam Adams and Patrick Henry. There is no
doubt that these gentlemen were finished agitators, but they
hardly dared mention independence before 1776. American
nationalism was a product of the Revolution, not its cause.
The colonists, unlike the Irish, had no historic grievances or
anti-English tradition. Indeed, we find Irish and German
names among the loyalists who fought for the king, as among
the patriots who supported Washington; and several revolu-
tionary leaders, such as Tom Paine, were English-born.

Other modern historians have called it a class upheaval,
a social revolution of democracy against aristocracy. There
is something to be said for this. Pennsylvania was pushed
into the independence movement by frontier farmers, against
the wishes of the more prosperous Quakers and Germans.
But in North Carolina probably a majority of the frontiers-
men were Tory, out of hatred for the Whig oligarchy that
ruled the colony.

If the American Revolution was not caused by
democracy, it released it; and for that reason, most of the
poorer colonists joined the movement. Instinctively they felt
that, once Crown officials were out of the way, it would be
easier to deal with local bosses. Democracy had few sympa-
thizers, however, and no representatives among the revolu-
tionary leaders. George Washington, John Hancock, John
Jay, the Lees, Otises, Randolphs, Carrolls, Morrises, and
Pinckneys—all were among the wealthiest men in the colonies. From their point of view, the Revolution was simply
a political protest of Englishmen against being ruled by other
Englishmen. They therefore exhausted every attempt at
compromise before coming out for absolute separation, and
many of their relatives and friends took the king's side. Colonial merchants found it hard to choose between interference

in their business by English politicians or by local snooping committees, but in the end most of them followed their customers.

Independence, then, was a common goal for radical and conservative patriots, who naturally split when independence was attained and democracy demanded something more than a place in the chorus. As an Otis lamented in 1837, "You and I did not imagine, when the first war with Britain was over, that revolution was just begun!" It could not have been otherwise. The Declaration of Independence appealed to the deepest instincts of liberty and equality, and the men who fought would not be denied by those who led.

If Americans had really been as united and determined as the ringing phrases of the Declaration of Independence suggest, they could have achieved independence within a year. For the English were halfhearted in the war; the liberal Whigs made no secret of their sympathy with the rebels; and the English nation had no military leaders worthy of her tradition. We had the advantage of fighting on our own soil, while the English had to transport troops and supplies by slow and precarious sailing vessels, at an expense tripled by the prevailing corruption. But Congress found it very difficult to keep an army together. Americans were willing to turn out as militia and repel an invasion of their own state; but only the very patriotic, or the very poor, or the Irish, could be induced to stay in the regular army.

The United States would not have achieved its independence but for the leadership of George Washington, one of the best and greatest men in recorded history. His patience in dealing with an undisciplined and jealous people, his firmness in adversity and moderation in victory, his wholehearted devotion to the cause, and his utter carelessness of self carried the colonies through the crucial years of war.

Even so, independence could not have been won without the help of France. Louis XVI and his ministers, eager to avenge the defeats of the last war and captivated by Ben Franklin, gave unneutral aid to the United States from the beginning and became its ally in 1778. Holland and Spain then joined up, and the War of American Independence extended to European waters and the Far East. A perfect cooperation between Washington's American army, Rochambeau's French expeditionary force, and the fleet of the Comte de Grasse brought about the surrender of Lord Cornwallis at Yorktown in 1781 which led to the end of the war.

Great things were now expected of the Americans by their friends, the European liberals. The thirteen colonies, in becoming the thirteen states, swept out royalty, titles, established churches, and primogeniture. The most generous and liberal principles of government and society were, it seemed, engraved on their statutes. They were a simple nation of farmers, and the resources of a new country would keep them from want. What an opportunity to renounce wealth, power, and all the vain pomps of the Old World, to devote their youthful energies to letters, the fine arts, and the search for absolute truth in government, religion, and philosophy—in short, to play the role that Greece had taken in the ancient world! But America was not a sterile country like Greece; and her people, most of whom had emigrated to better their condition in life, could not rest content with plain living and high thinking while a rich continent, ready to exploit, lay at their back doors.

In government, the Americans did better than their most ardent admirers hoped. The principles enunciated in the Declaration of Independence: "that all men are created equal, that they are endowed by their Creator with certain unalienable Rights, that among these are Life, Liberty and the pursuit of Happiness. That to secure these rights, Governments are instituted among Men, deriving their just powers from the consent of the governed"—these ideas had been the current coin of speculation since the later Roman Empire. The principles of the Virginia Bill of Rights—freedom of speech and of the press, trial by law, and the judgment of one's peers—went back to the Great Charter of 1215. But no government had yet been founded on those principles.

It was not difficult for the Americans to create workable *state* governments, for they had only to take the corporate form of colonial government to which they were accustomed, lop off the royal officials, and add a bill of rights. All the state constitutions of that period have been replaced or radically amended, but their defects were in detail rather than in principle.

Federal government was a different and far more difficult problem, for the people had no intention of parting with powers they had won from king and parliament. The first federal constitution, the Articles of Confederation (ratified 1781), worked well for a league of states at war, but very ill for a government in time of peace. All powers of taxation, for instance, were left to the states, which honored or neglected the requisitions of Congress as they saw fit. Congress could not compel them to observe the treaty of peace, which gave England an excuse to retain garrisons on United States soil and thus to exert pressure on the states. Yet the Articles of Confederation might have developed into an efficient government, if amendment had not required unanimous consent of the states.

In 1783 the United States was in an economic situation like that of the new nations of Europe in 1919 and the new nations of Asia in 1945. It took time to find substitutes for protected trade within the British Empire. Even former allies were entrenched within high tariff walls. Agricultural produce fell to almost nothing for want of a foreign market. The abundant specie left behind by French and British armies went to Europe for luxuries, which people always crave after a long war. Merchants of the seacoast towns, having exhausted their credit in Europe, began to distrain on their rural debtors. Thousands of farmers lost their land through lawsuits or were thrown into jail for debt. Some states relieved them by scaling down debts by act of legislature or by issuing paper money, which quickly depreciated.

In Massachusetts, controlled by merchants and creditors, the farmers' situation became so desperate that it broke out in Shays's rebellion (1786-87). That particular upheaval was quickly suppressed, but not before threatening to break out elsewhere. Certain men of property were so frightened that they invited a German prince to try his hand at being king of America. The more thoughtful leaders believed that a strong federal government was needed to protect property from radical state laws, preserve order at home, and make the country respected abroad. Such was the cause and origin of the federal Constitution under which we still live.

The Constitution was drafted by a convention of states' delegates during the summer of 1787. Washington presided; Franklin lent his common sense; James Madison and James Wilson contributed a sound and scholarly knowledge of political science; Gouverneur Morris put on the final polish. The majority wanted as strong a government as they thought the people would stand, but there was much bickering and compromise among rival interests and sections. The Senate was established as a bulwark for minorities against majorities. The wide power of the president was meant to give his office energy and prestige, qualities which had been lacking in the weak state executives.

The essence of the Constitution, the unique principle which ensured its success, was the federal government's complete and compulsive operation on individuals. Unlike the older Confederation and the modern United Nations, which can touch the individual only through a member state and which depend on the governments of those states to enforce their decisions, the government of the United States operates directly, by its own courts and officials, on every person within the Union. Within its sphere of action the federal government is supreme, but that sphere is limited by the Constitution. The states retain all powers not expressly granted. No sharp line could be drawn between the two jurisdictions, although in due time the Supreme Court would piece out the pattern of one.

There was a keen contest in almost every state between the advocates and the opponents of ratification. The latter, the anti-federalists, appeared certain to win, for the Constitution violated almost every principle of government then popular. Radicals and democrats feared a presidential tyranny and disliked the prohibition of confiscatory laws (Article I, Section 10). Plain folk saw no reason why they should take power from their own state governments and give it to a Congress, almost as remote as the British Parliament, in which their states might be voted down. The propertied classes—the conservative wing of the patriots of '76—were organized and presented cogent arguments in tracts such as those in *The Federalist*. Yet even with this activity and the support of Washington and Franklin, it was only by sharp politics and the promise of a federal bill of rights that the federalists were able to get the Constitution adopted.

Washington's election as the first president of the United States did much to preserve the fruits of the Revolution and gave hope of stability and union. Danger to both would come less from the enemies of the Constitution than from its friends. Within a few years the anti-federalists had become the watchdogs of a Constitution which Hamilton and Morris regarded as a weak, temporary structure, unfit for periods of storm and stress. Time has proved how very wrong they were.

CHAPTER THREE

Integration: 1789-1815

In 1783 a few hundred mutinous soldiers drove the government of the United States from its capital. Ten years later the federal government promptly suppressed a "Whiskey Rebellion" in western Pennsylvania and forced even the mountain moonshiners to pay federal excise. That difference is a fair test of what the new Constitution and President Washington accomplished.

During Washington's presidency (1789-97), the federal judiciary was established and given power to hear appeals in all cases involving conflicts between federal and state jurisdiction. Congress, adopting the advice of Alexander Hamilton, the brilliant young secretary of the treasury, funded the war debt, which was paid off within a generation. Peace with honor was preserved during a great European war. England and Spain were induced to relinquish the forts they held on our western territory. The West was convinced that she was better off in the Union than out. Yet for all that, the "father of his country" went out of office under a storm of criticism such as few presidents have suffered. For the two-party system had sprung up.

Washington accepted Hamilton's financial advice because he wished to pay the debts and vindicate the good name of his country. Hamilton looked much further. Despising human nature, he believed that the Union could not endure unless it created privilege. Lacking the power to confer orders and titles, the federal government must wave a magic wand over paper values, protect shipping and industry, and

26

thus earn the solid loyalty of the businessmen. The life of the average rough-necked American—a little crude farming, much hunting and loafing—disgusted Hamilton. He wished to help "big" men to "develop" the national resources, so that the little men could become their workers.

Hamilton's financial system (funding, assumption, protection, Bank of the United States) was intrinsically sound but politically weak. Its immediate benefits fell largely to the North, which owned most of the shipping and most of the government securities. There was little advantage for the southern planters, who had the traditional farmer's antagonism to financiers and banks. The Virginia gentry, deep readers in political theory, sanctioned this prejudice by a prevailing economic doctrine—that agriculture was the sole source of wealth, and bankers mere lice on the farmer's body.

As early as 1790, the Virginia legislature protested that Hamilton's schemes were unauthorized by the Constitution. Here was the first whisper of the doctrine of states' rights. Then and thereafter, states' rights has been merely a device to prevent the majority in Congress from abusing its power. It has been invoked to defend free speech from suppression (1798), to protect the shipping interest (1809-14), to promote free trade against protection (1832), to defend slavery from abolition (1837-61), alcohol from prohibition (1920-33), and white supremacy against the rights of Negroes (1954-?). Every state in turn has declared her own absolute sovereignty, only to denounce as treasonable similar declarations by other states. Every majority party has yelled for nationalism when in the saddle and for states' rights when thrown.

In Thomas Jefferson, Washington's secretary of state, the opposition found an ideal leader. Jefferson thought well of human nature. A fastidious gentleman, an architect and writer of distinction, he believed firmly in the capacity of the people to govern, provided they were educated and as long as a majority of them lived by farming. Not ambition but a fundamental divergence of purpose caused his breach with Hamilton. Behind their wrangle over actual policy lay two opposite conceptions of what America was and might be: the Roman and the Greek. Hamilton, the Roman, thought in terms of union, wealth, and power; Jefferson, the Greek, in terms of beauty, simplicity, and liberty.

In the presidential election of 1792, several southern states voted for George Clinton (the Alfred E. Smith of that day) instead of John Adams, for vice-president. Jefferson had formed a working alliance with a New York faction whose cleverest member, Aaron Burr, was learning how to use the Tammany Society for political ends. Parties have come and gone—but the Democratic party still straddles, somewhat unsteadily, the gap between Tammany and the South; and the Republicans of today, heirs to the Hamiltonian tradition, are the favorite party of business and finance.

The rise of an opposition was deplored by Washington, and Madison lent his hand to the process only because he feared the republic was in danger. Political parties were in bad odor at that time, owing to their current, corrupt practices in England and it was feared that they might destroy a Constitution which seemed to leave no place for their operation. Yet we can see now that, without national political parties, the Union would not have lasted a generation. Unless held to her fellow states by party bonds, the first state injured in pride or interest by federal legislation would have seceded from the Union. With parties in action, practical politicians seeking to win national elections have been forced to reconcile rival interests and sections on their platforms. Their so-called timidity in attempting to ignore popular issues such as slavery, religion, and civil rights has really been a form of wisdom; for once an issue of that nature divides the nation along sectional or class lines, civil war or social violence is likely to follow. Yet parties can neglect issues that interest the people only at the risk of losing popular support. So there you are!

While the great mass of people were still unattached to either the Hamiltonian Federalists or the Jeffersonian Republicans, France established her government as a republic and declared war against England. This situation immediately revealed two opposing forces in American foreign policy that were active for 150 years: the vertical force, tending to isolation, and the horizontal force, tending to participation in world affairs. The latter, obviously, has won out. One of the professed reasons for the Revolution was to place America outside the European balance of power, with its endless succession of wars. Yet every European war that involves some principle dear to American hearts has pulled us back in.

The great question in 1793—whether the United States would support the French or the British brand of liberty, or remain neutral to both—crystallized the two parties that were in process of formation. The Federalists, valuing their commercial relations with the mother country and regarding French Jacobinism as a menace to government, property, and morality, became strongly pro-British. They remained so even during the War of 1812 between England and the United States. The Republicans, on the other hand, believing that France had taken up the torch of progress and hating England as a nest of privilege and attractive corruption, became pro-French to the point of siding against their own government in a conflict with that power.

It was this excessive partisanship that Washington flayed in his Farewell Address. In 1793 he had declared the neutrality of the United States towards the European war and had prevented the envoy of Republican France from using American ports to fit out privateers and filibustering expeditions. This was much too cool for the Republicans, who pointed out that France had done for us in 1776 what Washington denied to her in 1793. The British, in the meantime, managed to hurt their American partisans by high-handed seizures of American ships.

Washington could have had war with England in 1794 at the drop of a hat; but he wanted peace at almost any price in order to give the Union time to "set." John Jay, sent on a special mission to England, concluded a treaty which settled all pressing questions but made such slight concessions to American commerce that Washington required all his influence and sacrificed most of his popularity to obtain the consent of the Senate. He was well justified, for Jay's treaty secured British evacuation of our northern frontier posts and, indirectly, the opening of the Mississippi to the down-river trade of western pioneers.

Since Washington refused to accept a third term, the Federalists nominated John Adams in 1796; the Republicans, Thomas Jefferson. Adams won by a narrow majority and found a contest with France on his hands. In retaliation for Jay's treaty, the French Republic encouraged her privateers to prey upon American ships. A special mission that Adams sent to France was dismissed with threats and demands for money. When the news reached America, there was an outbreak of popular indignation: "Millions for defense, but not one cent for tribute."

This was just the opportunity the Federalists wanted to discredit the pro-French Republicans, draw closer to England, and strengthen the federal government. Congress, swept off its feet, built a navy and revived the Marine Corps, greatly increased the army, inaugurated naval hostilities with France, abrogated the "entangling alliance" of 1778, and passed a Sedition Act to suppress political criticism. Old wives' tales about secret conspiracies against religion, morality, and government, which in all times are used by rascals to arouse honest citizens against sincere liberals, were warmed up to "prove" the Republicans to be fellow travelers of the French Jacobins.

Hamilton got himself appointed head of the army and planned to conquer New Orleans, if not Mexico, from France's ally, Spain. In 1799 President Adams, suspecting Hamilton's project, thwarted it by sending a new peace mission to France. Then reaction set in. The Republicans convinced thousands of voters that the Federalist brand of patriotism was a mere pretext for tyranny, and Jefferson won the presidential election of 1800-1801.

Jefferson's inaugural address was a confession of democratic faith. His ideal was "a wise and frugal government, which shall restrain men from injuring one another, shall leave them otherwise free to regulate their own pursuits of industry and improvement, and shall not take from the mouth of labor the bread it has earned." To this ideal he remained true. Congress at his suggestion repealed taxes and cut down appropriations, dismantled the navy, reduced the army, and kept out of foreign entanglements. No attempt was made to restrain the violent attacks of the Federalist press.

In order to secure the West an outlet, Jefferson bargained with France for New Orleans and, through the caprice of Napoleon, obtained Louisiana—the vast territory between the Mississippi and the Rocky Mountains. Jefferson's wisdom and moderation were rewarded in 1804: in his campaign for re-election, he won the vote of every state but two.

The renewal of war between England and France gave Jefferson an unhappy second term. Each tried to prevent neutrals from trading with the other, and the Royal Navy revived the unpleasant practice of impressing seamen from American ships. Jefferson, after trying to steer his way between the contending powers, commanded American ships and seamen to stay at home and avoid trouble. This embargo of fifteen months (1807-9), instead of bringing England and France to terms, pleased their shipowners but ruined many of ours. It also gave new life to the dying Federalist party and started it on the road of states' rights to defend the northern shipping interests.

Yet despite this mistake, Jefferson was one of our greatest presidents. His principles were sometimes too high for practical politics; but he preferred compromise to coercion, and like Franklin he regarded the worst peace as better than the best war. He salvaged for future generations the purest ideals of the American Revolution—simplicity, democracy, and individual liberty. Indeed, no one in modern times has approached so near as Jefferson to Plato's ideal of the philosopher-statesman: a man in whom the power of thought and the power of action are perfectly balanced; a man conscious of the past, equal to the present, and reaching forward into the future.

James Madison succeeded Jefferson in 1809. His first administration is a story of drifting into war; the second, of war itself. Madison had the fatal delusion of clever diplomacy. If England had accepted the opening he offered in 1809, the War of 1812 would have come earlier and against France. But Napoleon took that trick and the next by pretending to revoke his decrees against neutral trade. An act of Congress forbidding commercial intercourse with Great Britain found that country in a desperate situation. In June 1812 she announced the repeal of most of her obnoxious regulations, but it was too late to prevent war. A new generation was in control of Congress—young men like Clay and Calhoun, many of them westerners, who burned to conquer Canada and thus settle our accounts with England once and for all. Before news of the British concession arrived, Congress had declared war. "On to Canada" was the cry.

Canada, however, obtained most of the glory from this war. Thinly settled and ill-garrisoned by a mother country at grips with Napoleon, she was able to beat off four separate invasions in 1812 and to force one United States army to surrender at Detroit. Our success in naval duels (*Constitution* vs. *Guerriere, Hornet* vs. *Peacock,* etc.) was some consolation, but we failed to shake English control of the sea. In 1813, largely through Perry's victory on Lake Erie, we recovered our lost territory; but the next year, Napoleon's fall released British veterans for American operations. Two formidable attacks on our Niagara and Lake Champlain fronts were repelled; but in August a British expeditionary force landed in Chesapeake Bay, marched unopposed to within sight of Washington, routed a rabble of militia, and burned the Capitol and the White House.

In that dark hour for the Union, the Federalists of New England summoned a convention of state delegates at Hartford. Jefferson's embargo had convinced the trading Yankees that the government was in the hands of their enemies. The War of 1812 appeared to them unnecessary and immoral, when England was upholding the liberty of nations against the tyrant Napoleon. The New England Federalists therefore picked up states' rights, the stone Hamilton had rejected, and hurled it at Madison, who had employed the same weapon against the Sedition Act in 1798. Three New England states withheld or recalled their militia from federal service. There was open talk of seceding from the Union and forming a Northern Confederacy; if there had not been a staunch Republican minority in New England, and if the Federalist leaders had not been wiser than their press, secession might well have been attempted. As it was, the Hartford Convention proved a mere safety valve for discontent. It adjourned after passing some harmless resolutions in favor of states' rights and against the administration.

Early in January 1815, Andrew Jackson won a brilliant victory at New Orleans which took the sting out of our earlier defeats. Two weeks earlier, the treaty of peace had been signed at Ghent, Belgium. This treaty settled none of the pre-war disputes, for the British refused to recede an inch in impressment and neutral rights; but the war taught them for the first time to treat us with respect, while the United States learned that Canada would fight for imperial integrity. In 1817 both governments agreed to the epoch-making naval disarmament on the Great Lakes. Boundary and other disputes were cleared up in subsequent negotiations.

An era of American history ends in 1815, the year of world peace. The federal government, having weathered a war, was firmly established. Confident in their power to lick all creation, the Americans turned their backs on Europe and faced west.

CHAPTER FOUR

Democracy: 1815-1848

The ten years after the Peace of Ghent were the halcyon days of the republic—the "era of good feelings," as it was called. The Jeffersonian Republican party, learning wisdom with power, appropriated one by one the nationalist policies of Hamilton and left the Federalists nothing to stand on but a very bad war record. Madison completed his second term and was succeeded by his secretary of state, James Monroe, also of Virginia. Monroe governed eight years and was succeeded by *his* secretary of state, John Quincy Adams of Massachusetts.

By that time, things had happened which made the people want a change both of men and of measures. New issues continued to arise until a great Civil War had been fought, in which some of them were settled.

The leading statesmen of the country in 1815—Clay, Calhoun, Adams, and Webster—were of the generation that had grown up since the Revolution. Ardent nationalists, they were somewhat fearful of the rapid expansion that was creating new states and conflicting interests. As they saw it, the proper way to forestall a clash of sections was to stimulate an American spirit by the sort of legislation that would cater to everybody—Hamilton's old formula, somewhat broadened. Accordingly, Congress passed the first protective tariff in 1816, chartered a new United States Bank on the model of Hamilton's, undertook to construct a section of what is now known as the National Highway, and passed a navigation act to protect the merchant marine. When some of these laws were challenged on the ground that Congress had exceeded its constitutional power, Chief Justice Marshall and the Supreme Court invariably upheld them as reasonable and proper exercises of federal power. Yet none of these measures long persisted in federal policy.

The one permanent result of the new nationalism was John Quincy Adams' doctrine of "Hands off America!" to which he induced President Monroe to put his name in 1823. It was a warning to Europe against intervention in Latin America, and to Russia against expanding from Alaska along the Oregon coast. Every previous declaration of American foreign policy had been the subject of violent contention, but there was little criticism of Monroe's message, even though many Americans were more eager to help the Greeks win their independence than to protect the Latin Americans in theirs.

The real reason why the country acquiesced in nationalism at this time was simple: America was changing so fast that the different sections did not yet know what their dominant interests would be. By 1825, when President John Quincy Adams proposed more paternalistic legislation, the sections had acquired new interests and the movement toward national integration had halted.

We cannot understand the complex events that led to the Civil War—and thus to the America of today—without knowing something of the vital forces that determined them: westward expansion, industrialism, humanitarianism, and democracy.

(1) Westward expansion had been going on ever since the colonies were founded, and had begun to gather momentum in 1796; but the speed greatly accelerated after 1815, when the Indian tribes north of the Ohio and south of Ten-

nessee were no longer able to resist. New methods of transportation made migration easier and linked the settlers with markets for their farm produce. By 1815 the flat-bottom, stern-wheel river steamboat was common on the western rivers, creeks, and bayous—as Lincoln said, "wherever the ground was a little damp."

As long as the rivers determined lines of trade and emigration, the western pioneers were confined largely to a distinct breed which, for want of a better term, we call the upland southern stock. It was composed largely of two groups: descendants of those eighteenth-century immigrants who had followed the folds of the Appalachian Mountains southwesterly from Pennsylvania, and bond servants who were set free in the southern states. These strains mingled their blood in Kentucky and Tennessee and spread out fanwise as soon as the Indians were put in their "proper" places—under ground.

Abraham Lincoln and Jefferson Davis, for instance, were both of this stock. They were born in Kentucky log cabins during the same year. Abe was taken by his father to Indiana and completed his growth in Illinois; Jeff went with his parents to Mississippi and became a southern planter. Both, however, were exceptional men of their class, or of any class.

The southern uplander at his best was a magnificent pioneer: courageous, generous, hospitable; but more than any other American type he was unprogressive, illiterate, superstitious, violent, and intolerant. He mastered the technique of subduing the wilderness, but seldom ventured beyond the woods that afforded him game, housing, fencing, and fuel. His agriculture was incredibly crude. He tolerated slavery because it "kept the nigger in his place," but disliked Negroes, slaveholders, and Yankees with equal intensity. In the backwoods of Tennessee, Arkansas, and the lower South, the southern uplander remains today much as he was in 1825.

The West also attracted southern lowlanders of gentler

strain, but too few to exert much influence on the growing West, compared with the horde of Yankees and Germans that came pouring in during the 1830's and 1840's. This northern migration to the West was helped by the Erie Canal, completed by New York State in 1825. It made New York City the metropolis of the East, the principal gateway to the West, and the leading market for western products. Connecting with the Great Lakes at Buffalo, the Erie provided a cheap water route for immigrants to—and bulky products from—the hitherto unpeopled northern regions of Ohio, Indiana, and Illinois, where feeder canals were constructed. These were later extended to Michigan and Wisconsin, and by 1845 railroads began to parallel the canals.

With the Yankee inundation, the Middle West, which had been closely allied with Virginia politics, began to gravitate toward New England. In 1856 the Yankees cemented, in the Republican party, a sectional alliance that has endured ever since.

(2) Industrialism was the second leading force. In the northeastern states, from Maine to Ohio and Maryland, it took two forms: a factory system, and a half-way stage in which the worker made up goods at home from materials furnished by the capitalist. In the South it took the form of the cotton plantation. During Jefferson's embargo and the War of 1812, when New England politicians were crying ruin, their more thrifty constituents were harnessing water power to factories for the making of textiles, paper, glass, hardware, and hundreds of other products. New York, New Jersey, and Pennsylvania also fell into the industrial belt. All these "infant industries" wanted protection from the products of England, where manufacturing technique was more highly developed.

The alliance of industry with banking made a combination that thrust the farming and shipping interests of the

East into the background. This movement contributed to the growth of cities, created many new ones (such as Lowell and Rochester, where water power was available), and attracted thousands of immigrants from the British Isles and Germany. Social evils followed, as in England; but not of the same magnitude, for there was less economic compulsion. Feeling no need to accept and regulate the new industrial order, as Europe was beginning to do, Americans tried to escape it by migrating westward or by experimenting with co-operation and communism.

(3) Humanitarianism was also an important force of the period. The trade-union movement, begun in the 1820's, was led astray by reformers in search of their several utopias; but other reformers brought a notable advance in law, education, and the treatment of the poor and unfortunate. Practical men of vision such as Horace Mann, supported by the labor unions and the new voters, imposed the principle of free compulsory public education on almost all the northern states. High-speed printing and cheap newspapers, public libraries and popular lyceums, diffused knowledge if not wisdom. Special institutions were provided for the blind and for deaf mutes; imprisonment for debt was abolished; and some of the insane were placed in asylums. Another group of reformers, the abolitionists, resolved to remove the foul blot of slavery from American soil.

At the time of the Revolution, slavery had existed in every state of the Union; but in all except South Carolina and Georgia, it was generally regarded as inhumane, unrepublican, and temporary. The northern states, at relatively slight cost, abolished slavery by 1804; but the South naturally shrank from a reform that would upset its planting system and leave a stupendous free Negro problem. In addition, the cotton gin had given slavery a new lease on life by making possible a westward expansion of the cotton-growing area. After the

War of 1812, planters invaded the rich black belts of Alabama, Mississippi, southern Tennessee, and even Missouri.
Their traditions were transmitted, in a somewhat diluted
and romantic form, to thousands of enterprising backwoods-
men and immigrant Yankees, who purchased a slave or two
on credit, saved up the proceeds of a few crops, acquired a
plantation, sent their sons to college, and founded a new
family of southern gentlemen.

As early as 1819, when there was a fierce debate in Congress as to whether Missouri should enter the Union slave
or free, a defensive attitude toward slavery was discernible
behind southern politics. Slave owners began to reflect
that since Congress had assumed the power to build roads
and charter banks, it might also attempt to free the slaves
whenever the North obtained a majority. And the North
was growing faster than the South, primarily because it attracted the European immigrants. As a result, there was a
marked reaction in the South from the nationalism of 1812
to the states' rights furor of 1860.

The southern slave-owning class was marked by many
gradations, ranging from Robert E. Lee to the backwoods
bully; but in the main, the plantation developed a fine type
of gentleman—generous, public spirited, responsible. His
great, though natural, error was in regarding slavery as a permanent necessity rather than a temporary expedient. His
apparent finality on the subject stimulated a new and radical abolitionist movement in the North, led by William Lloyd
Garrison and Theodore Weld. This movement irritated the
southerner and, in time, created a southern national feeling.

The poor whites and the non-slaveholders, although
envious of their gentry, agreed with them that slavery was
the only possible status for the Negro. Anyone who disagreed
was forced to leave the South, for criticism of the system was
forbidden by law and suppressed by public opinion. Educa-

tion was withheld from the poor white as from the black; literature and the new humanity found no foothold; and the southern intellect, so fruitful in the era of Jefferson, was now devoted to defending an institution which the civilized world regarded with increasing horror. Southern statesmen, professors, and even ministers of the gospel prepared their people for a tragic destiny by teaching them that Negro slavery was the foundation of their prosperity, the cornerstone of their society, the palladium of liberty, and the law of God.

(4) Democracy was a fourth great force of this age. Western pioneers from Michigan to Mississippi made their new constitutions responsive to the fleeting popular will. The disfranchised in the northeastern states then demanded and got the vote. The rapidly increasing numbers of Irish and German immigrants were quickly naturalized and inducted into the Democratic party. A great mass of ignorant voters offered new opportunities to professional politcians for power and corruption. Political technique had to be revised to catch the passions of the multitude, and candidates were lucky if they had been born in a log cabin.

Yet this political democracy was a very natural result of equal opportunity; and the crude, boisterous political tactics of the day reflected the gusto and vigor of a youthful people beginning to feel their power. European radicals and republicans pointed to America with pride, and their rulers regarded the great republic much as she later came to view Russia: as a foul nest of bad principles, the more dangerous because they appeared to be successful. In Canada and Mexico, American democrats proved more able and dangerous propagandists than have the Russian Communists of our day.

Democracy carried Andrew Jackson into the White House in 1829. The hero of New Orleans was an upstanding frontier leader—self-educated, impulsive, a terror to horse thieves, Indians, Britishers, and other "varmints." The

South rallied to him as a slaveholder; the new democratic politicians of the North picked him as a leader who would reward friends and punish enemies; and the westerners voted for him as a man of their own sort.

Jackson was the first military man since Washington to be elected president. The qualities which commended him to the voters were the opposite of those which made Washington something more than a military leader. Yet he made a good president. Although quick to anger, he settled controversies with foreign countries that had baffled John Quincy Adams. He smote financial privilege when it appeared in the shape of the United States Bank. He enhanced the prestige of the presidency, as a sort of tribune of the people, while his own success assured the common man that family and education were not necessary for election to the highest office in the republic. On the other hand, it seemed obvious to him that any good American who voted right was fit for any position in the civil service. His introduction of the spoils system into the federal government was highly approved by the victors.

The most instructive episode of Jackson's presidency was the nullification mix-up with South Carolina. That state was suffering from the competition of new cotton plantations in Alabama and Mississippi, but her planters blamed their poverty on the protective tariff. They concluded that protection was unconstitutional; and their leading statesman, John C. Calhoun, father of the tariff of 1816, had a change of heart. This somber man of flinty logic welded the loose notions of states' rights, with which earlier politicians had played, into a complete system.

Calhoun was not consciously a disunionist; he was trying to *prevent* the disunion that was certain to come if the Hamilton-Clay formula of nationalist legislation persisted. In practice, he felt, nationalism had proved to be mere sectional tyranny. The only way, he thought, to keep the states united was to reduce federal power to the lowest terms any one state found in accordance with its interests. Federal policy would be shaped, not by multiple sectional interests, but by their highest common factors. It was either that or government by give-and-take; and South Carolina, having taken all she wanted, would not give.

Nullification, which Calhoun deduced from the sovereignty of the states, was the right of any state to refuse obedience to any act of Congress it considered unconstitutional, and to secede from the Union if the other states objected. South Carolina put this theory into practice against the high protective tariff of 1832. A state convention declared the tariff unconstitutional, null and not binding, and threatened to take over forcibly the United States customhouse at Charleston.

One ounce of Jackson's common sense was worth all Calhoun's logic. In a ringing proclamation, he exposed the absurdity of a state remaining in the Union and claiming its privileges while presuming to disobey federal laws. He was ready for a showdown, but Henry Clay's diplomacy prevented this. Congress substituted a compromise tariff with a sliding scale downward for that of 1832, and South Carolina repealed her ordinance of nullification. The principle of federal supremacy was sustained, but at a price. From 1835 to 1861, America was practically a free-trade country; and Calhoun devoted his gloomy talent to creating a solid South which would swing presidential elections with western support, or secede if she did not.

These events and movements in the East, West, and South determined a new political alignment. Around Jackson was formed a party that took the name Democratic and claimed direct descent from Jefferson. Jackson's opponents rallied around the gallant personality of Henry Clay and, in

1834, took the name Whig. In composition these new parties were more national than the old Republicans and Federalists or the later Democrats and Republicans, to which they roughly correspond. Both contained nationalist and states' rights elements; both contested every state in the Union and ardently wooed the growing West.

The Democrats were strongest among the southern uplanders and non-slaveholders, as well as in New York and Pennsylvania, where Martin Van Buren and James Buchanan had risen to power with an enlarged electorate. They controlled most of the immigrants. The Whigs, like the Federalists, were the party of property and respectability, big bankers and wealthy planters, although they endeavored to conceal the fact by democratic slogans and tactics. As Emerson wrote, the Democrats had the best cause, the Whigs the best men. It was the ambition of the leading Whigs—Clay, Webster, Seward, Toombs, and A. H. Stevens—to form a great national conservative party, like the English Tories, which would protect the major interest of every section and preserve the Union. But the Democrats, aggressive and positive, with a certain instinct for the popular will, kept the Whigs on the defensive. The latter won only two presidential elections (1840 and 1848) and never acquired the organic unity of their rivals.

Both parties adopted at their birth the convention method of nominating candidates (a great help to professional politicians) and the spoils system of rewarding party workers. Both developed a campaign technique—stump speaking, spellbinding, political clubs, rallies, barbecues, and joint debates—that afforded entertainment to the people in those simple times. Everyone then voted the straight ticket. At the first Democratic national convention, in 1835, the two-thirds rule was adopted in order to strengthen Van Buren's nomination. The same necessity that made every party platform a compromise between sectional interests led to the frequent nomination of colorless presidential candidates. From Van Buren to Taft, the country obtained a great president only by accident.

President Van Buren (1837-41) dealt in a statesmanlike way with foreign complications and with the situation created by a financial panic. But no administration, whatever its ability, can remain popular when business is bad and the farmers are discontented. In 1840 the Whigs nominated a retired general, William Henry Harrison, and won the western vote by a rollicking log-cabin, hard-cider campaign. But their triumph was short-lived. Harrison died a month after his inauguration; Vice-President Tyler quarrelled with his party; and in 1844 the Democrats won back the West and the presidency with the slogans "Reannexation of Texas" and "Reoccupation of Oregon." For the westward movement had passed beyond United States territory into a province of Mexico and leapt the Great Plains to the Pacific.

Oregon (which then included Washington, Idaho, and British Columbia) had been jointly occupied by British and United States fur traders under a treaty of 1818. Reports of the mighty forests, equable climate, and rich soil of this country reached the Middle West about 1840. Swarms of emigrants made the 2,000-mile journey in covered wagons over the Oregon Trail and formed communities along the lower Columbia River. England offered to divide the Oregon country by the Columbia. The Democratic party insisted on the whole of it ("Fifty-four forty or fight"), but was glad to compromise on the forty-ninth parallel when at war with Mexico (1846).

Americans began to cross the border into Texas in the 1820's by invitation of the Mexican government. As the land was fertile and the climate adapted for cotton, it attracted southern slaveholders and the rougher sort of pioneer who could not get on with proud Mexicans. Texas declared her independence of Mexico in 1836 and, after a sharp conflict, became the Lone Star Republic. She really wanted annexation to the United States, but the northern states repelled this because it would mean another (and a vast) slave state. For the same reason, the south wanted Texas in. The deadlock was broken, and Texas was admitted to the Union on March 3, 1845.

James K. Polk, the dark horse who won the presidential election in 1844, was a go-getter. His first ambition was to acquire California from Mexico before England or France could take it. Since Mexico would not sell, he ordered American troops into debatable border territory along the Rio Grande. When the touchy Mexicans defended themselves, Congress declared that war existed by act of Mexico (April 1846).

The southern as well as the northern Whigs opposed the Mexican War as aggressive, unnecessary, and certain to bring internal complications. It was popular only in the West. Backwoods militiamen were eager to "revel in the halls of the Montezumas" and the regular army, under Taylor and Scott, fought a way in for them. For a time it looked as though strutting democracy would usurp the throne of Montezuma and annex the whole of Mexico, but Polk decided to insist only on the cession of Texas, New Mexico, and California to the United States (1848).

At the conclusion of this highly successful war, Americans were more pleased with themselves than ever before or since. "Manifest destiny" pointed to Canada and Cuba, Panama and the North Pole. Little they reckoned on the ultimate cost. When next the shotted cannon spoke, it was in a brothers' war.

CHAPTER FIVE

Dissolution: 1848-1877

Even before the Mexican War was finished, a squabble broke out over the plunder. Tension between anti-slavery and pro-slavery, North and South, broke through party lines and threatened the Union.

Calhoun insisted that slavery follow the American flag. The southern states, he claimed, as joint owners of the new territory, had as much right to transport their human chattels thither as northerners their household goods. Not that they wished to do so, for almost everyone imagined that California and New Mexico were unsuitable for slave labor, but the privilege must be allowed as a southern right. In other words, the United States must deliberately introduce slavery into soil already free.

Stated in this way, the proposal seemed monstrous to thousands of northerners. Out of their feeling came the Free-Soil party (1848), pledged to keep human bondage out of all territories of the United States.

Gold was discovered in California just after the war was over, and in 1849 thousands of adventurers came flocking in by overland trail and sailing ship, forming a picturesque but unruly population. Oregon had no law but voluntary compacts of the settlers; Utah was ruled by the theocracy led by Brigham Young, which was all very well for the Mormons but tough on the Gentiles. Yet for two years these growing territories were denied lawful government because Congress could not decide whether to give them the "privilege" of slavery. And the southern states called the Nashville Convention—sinister reminder of the Hartford Convention—to consider secession from a Union that discriminated against their property.

Finally, after a battle of giants in the Senate, Henry Clay got through the Compromise of 1850. Under its terms, California was admitted as a free state, and Oregon was organized as a free territory; the question as to whether slavery would be allowed in Utah and New Mexico was left, by implication, to their territorial legislatures; the domestic slave trade was prohibited in Washington, D.C.; and a new and drastic Fugitive Slave Law was passed in the hope of forcing northern states to give up runaways. The last provision was wholly a matter of principle: despite the abolitionist "underground railroad," the number of slaves who made good their escape was insignificant.

That Compromise of 1850 saved the Union for another ten years, but it split the Whig party. Northern anti-slavery Whigs, unable to stomach the Fugitive Slave Law, joined the Free-Soil party; the southern Whigs, disgusted with their northern colleagues, joined the Democrats. From 1852 to 1860, the Democrats formed a great national conservative party in which northerners presided and southerners directed.

For a time, slavery disappeared from politics, while North and South expanded along their divergent lines. Manufacturers prospered in spite of low Democratic tariffs, and the price of cotton rose. The American merchant marine reached its acme with the clipper ship, and Commodore Perry visited Japan. Railroads and the reaper opened up the big prairies of Illinois, Iowa, and Minnesota to Yankee, German, and Scandinavian immigrants. The Know-Nothing party, anti-foreign and anti-Catholic, flourished for a year and then succumbed, split on the slavery question.

Stephen A. Douglas, the "little giant" of Illinois, was

responsible for the revival of the slavery question. Fearful lest New Orleans, rather than Chicago, become the terminus of the first transcontinental railway—for a railroad could not be run across the Great Plains without a protecting government—he proposed in 1854 to organize the country west of Missouri and Iowa as the territories of Kansas and Nebraska. To win southern votes, he incorporated in the bill a clause permitting slavery in the territories if their legislatures so desired. The Kansas-Nebraska Bill thus repealed the Missouri Compromise of 1820, which excluded slavery absolutely from the territory north of 36° 30′.

Naturally this breach of sectional compromise infuriated many northerners. The first consequence was the formation of a new northern party (replacing the Free-Soil) which took the name Republican. The second was a miniature civil war in Kansas, where "border ruffians" from Missouri fought with "jayhawkers" from the Middle West for the paper privilege of admitting or excluding slaves whom no one wished to import. Again, as in 1850, it was a question of principle and prestige—the sort of question that precipitates great wars.

In the election of 1856, the Democratic candidate, James Buchanan, won; but the new Republicans, promising to exclude from the territories "those twin relics of barbarism, polygamy and slavery," carried most of the northern states. The Whigs disappeared as a party.

Shortly after Buchanan's inauguration, the Supreme Court tried its hand at settling the question of slavery in the territories. In a case involving the slave Dred Scott, it declared flatly for Calhoun's doctrine that the slavery prohibition in the Missouri Compromise was null and void. Slavery, said the Court, followed the flag. This decision gained votes for the Republican party, made the Fugitive Slave Law a dead letter, and roused a certain admiration for John Brown, who, moved by indignant pity, attempted to free the slaves by force and paid with his life.

Brown's raid in turn drew the white South together and gave wider currency to the secession propaganda that had been increasing in volume since 1844. For the South was at bay. Slavery, her fundamental institution, was outlawed by every civilized country except Brazil, Spain, and Russia. Northern population and wealth, and abolitionist ideas within that population, were lighting a wall of fire about her. Why not escape while there was yet time? There need be no risk. The world must dance to the tune of the power who held a monopoly of cotton.

The only hope of preserving the Union peaceably beyond 1861 was another Democratic victory. But in 1860 the Democratic party split on a mere hair, a few words which more or less affirmed slavery.

The Republican party in 1860 was a northern rather than a mere anti-slavery party. It had been formed to realize certain northern and western desires which had been balked by the southern wing of the Democrats and Whigs—protective tariff, river and harbor bills, a Pacific railroad, free homesteads for settlers, and the exclusion of slavery from the territories. The platform of 1860 appealed to idealists, pioneers, mill-owners, and wage-earners. Abraham Lincoln was nominated as the only candidate likely to carry the doubtful states of Illinois and Indiana. He obtained only a plurality of the popular vote, and hardly a ballot was cast for him in the south, but the Democratic split gave him a majority in the electoral college. For the first time since the Constitution was adopted, the federal government was captured by a purely sectional party. As many statesmen had predicted, the defeated section revolted.

In December 1860, as soon as Lincoln's election was certain, South Carolina formally seceded from the Union and declared herself an independent nation. Florida, Georgia, Alabama, Mississippi, and Texas followed her lead in January 1861. On February 8, a congress of their delegates formed the Confederate States of America, with a constitution differing little from that of the United States save in stressing states' rights and making slavery the cornerstone. The next day Jefferson Davis was chosen president of the Confederacy. On March 4, Abraham Lincoln was inaugurated president of the United States.

No president in our history was so little known at his inauguration or inspired so little confidence as Lincoln. He was frankly bewildered at the situation, and public opinion gave him no lead. His inaugural promise that the Republican party would not interfere with slavery in the states was received with jeers in the new Confederacy. William H. Seward, his experienced secretary of state, proposed to win the South back by picking a quarrel with England and France. Horace Greeley urged him to let the wayward sisters depart in peace, and the abolitionists were frankly delighted at their loss. Others proposed constitutional amendments affirming the Dred Scott decision; these Lincoln rejected as contrary to the platform on which he was elected.

Few would face the facts and admit that Union could only be restored by force. For the Confederates would have no more union with the North at any price. They were sick and tired of hearing their favorite institution decried in Congress, and themselves denounced in the abolitionist press as manstealers and ruffians. Conscious of southern unity and confident of their ability to maintain it against all the world, they had deliberately founded a new government to assert the supremacy of the white race and its right to property in men.

The northern tier of slave states viewed the question in a slightly different light. Reluctant to break with the Union,

they awaited the outcome of a delicate negotiation between
the Confederacy and Lincoln over Fort Sumter, the federal fortress in Charleston Harbor. South Carolina demanded
its evacuation. Lincoln hesitated a month in the hope that
forbearance would cool the secession frenzy; but in early
April 1861, against the advice of most of his cabinet, he ordered Fort Sumter to be reinforced.

Lincoln had an uncanny sense of timing—an intui-
tion for the point at which appeasement must stop. He had
realized that to abandon Fort Sumter would not bring the
cotton states back or keep Virginia in. Retreat would only
recognize secession as an accomplished fact and depress
Union sentiment in the North to a level from which it could
never be revived.

As soon as the Confederates heard of the approaching
reinforcement, they opened fire on Fort Sumter (April 12),
and the great Civil War began. This firing on the flag convinced the North that secession was merely another name
for treason and brought into action the nationalist sentiment
that had been slowly ripening for half a century. Lincoln
called for volunteers and declared a blockade of the Confederate coast. Virginia promptly joined the Southern Confederacy; North Carolina, Tennessee, and Arkansas followed.
Maryland, Kentucky, and Missouri were divided in sentiment and contributed as heartily to the southern as to the
Union armies, but their state governments remained loyal.

In general, men followed their states out, or stayed with
them in the Union. If the states were sovereign, as the South
claimed, the secession of one's state dissolved one's allegiance
to the United States. If Robert E. Lee was a traitor, so was
George Washington. Yet men from every state could be
found in both the Confederate and the Union armies, and
pro-Unionism was as much a thorn to Jefferson Davis as pro-
southern or "copperhead" feeling was to Lincoln. It was a

true civil war—a war between two forms of society which had aroused such passionate loyalty in their members that they could no longer coexist under the same government.

The South had every reason for confidence. She was less populous than the North and greatly inferior in material resources, but her people were more used to fighting, more united as on the defensive and led by some of the greatest military commanders in all history. President Davis, an experienced and upright statesman, was also a military man. (No one foresaw that this would prove a handicap.) Although mistaken in their belief that Yankees would not fight and that England would intervene to get cotton, the southerners convinced every military critic in Europe that they were certain to win. For the North had to conquer an extensive country and crush a proud people; the southerners had only to repel invasion, and independence was theirs.

Two factors alone made it possible for the North to hold on long enough for sea power and superior numbers to count —the sentiment of union, and Abraham Lincoln. The President, resisting every demand to make the war an abolitionist crusade or a Republican junket, placed it on the sole ground of restoring the union of the states; in so doing, he won the great majority of northerners, who would not have fought merely to free the slaves. By his inspired leadership, the North came to believe that not only the future of America but the prestige of free government everywhere was bound up with the preservation of the Union. He and they were right. A southern victory was prayed for by every enemy to freedom in Europe; the triumph of the Union helped more than any event since the American Revolution to vindicate democracy.

Lincoln's greatness unfolded as the war progressed, but even his initial fumbling served the country better than any of his cocksure critics could have done. There were two

necessary roads to victory: constricting the South by blockade, and defeating the southern armies. Congress was slow
to provide the means to make the blockade effective; and until
the end of 1862, Lincoln shared the belief of his people that
the capture of Richmond, the Confederate capital, would
end the war. Yielding to popular impatience, he ordered a
premature invasion of Virginia, which was defeated at Bull
Run (July 21, 1861). General George B. McClellan, whom
he then called to high command, spent eight months creating an army from a civilian mob, while the South wasted time
and the North fretted.

In April 1862, the Army of the Potomac began to move
on Richmond by the Yorktown Peninsula. A clever feint
at Washington by "Stonewall" Jackson caused panic at the
capital, and Lincoln recalled an army corps essential for Mc-
Clellan's success. Lee, who at this juncture received command of the Confederate Army of Northern Virginia, frus-
trated McClellan's purpose in the Seven Days' battles around
Richmond (June 26-July 1, 1862). Under great difficulties,
and with the help of the Union navy, McClellan saved his
army and the cause; but northern opinion could see only his
failure to take Richmond, and Lincoln had to supplant him
for the good of the cause. Lee and Jackson disposed of Mc-
Clellan's successor at the second Battle of Bull Run (August
30, 1862) and cleared the way for an invasion of the North.

A southern victory on northern soil would have come
very close to winning southern independence and would cer-
tainly have obtained European recognition. Napoleon III
was urging the British cabinet to a joint intervention. Lincoln, on his own initiative, reinstated McClellan, who then
forced Lee to retreat at the Battle of Antietam in Maryland.
Lincoln seized this occasion to issue his first Emancipation
Proclamation, declaring the slaves in rebel states forever
free. He won the support of European liberals and of the

British workingman, who, through all his sufferings from the cotton famine, stood stoutly for the cause of liberty. But the northern Democrats, denouncing the "niggers' war," gained many seats in the fall elections; and Lee, by smashing Burnside at Fredericksburg, made the great Proclamation, for the time being, a mere threat.

Although the most spectacular battles were in the Virginian theater of war, the military campaigns in the West were more decisive. If the northern armies and armored gunboats could win back the Mississippi, drive a wedge of Union territory between it and the Appalachians, and work around the southern end of the mountains into Lee's rear, all his victories would be fruitless. That is just what Generals Grant, Thomas, and Sherman, and Admirals Porter and Farragut, achieved in 1862-64. Lee once more invaded the North, where he was defeated at Gettysburg (July 1-3, 1863) but made good his retreat with his troops' morale unimpaired.

Grant's brilliant victory at Chattanooga the following November was the real turning point in the war. It opened a window to the Carolinas, showed Lincoln a soldier who would take responsibility and act, and earned the modest, forthright Grant an appointment as commanding general of the Union armies.

Yet Grant's next campaign, that of the Wilderness in Virginia, was a costly failure. After losing 50,000 men, he stood exactly where McClellan had been two years before, and Lee's numerically inferior army was still undefeated. Lee was even able to detach Jubal A. Early in a raid on Washington, which gave the President a sight of battle within an hour's horseback ride from the White House (July 12, 1864).

That was the moment when the paper dollar hit rock bottom and the North almost lost heart. A new draft was necessary, and the presidential election was approaching. The Democrats nominated General McClellan on a platform declaring the war a failure; the Republican National Committee became so panic-stricken that it talked of removing Lincoln from the ticket. Just in time, Sherman captured Atlanta and began his epic march to the sea, while Phil Sheridan spread destruction through the Shenandoah Valley. Lincoln won by a substantial though not overwhelming majority.

Lincoln's re-election took the heart out of the South. The Confederacy was not defeated merely by naval blockade and superior numbers. She still had sufficient manpower in 1864 to keep up the war for years, if her will to fight had lasted. Three-quarters of the immense Union army was employed in guarding lines of communication and in garrison duty. Surmounting every difficulty, the South was producing sufficient arms and munitions; her printing presses turned out money enough to run the government; and scarcity of food existed only locally.

The planters, the women, and the government were still undaunted, but the poor whites began to call it "a rich man's war and a poor man's fight." Confederate armies dwindled more by desertion than by defeat. As a surrendered "Johnny Reb" replied to a boastful "Yank" at Appomattox, "You-all never licked us. We-all got plumb tired out lickin' you-all!"

When Sherman rolled up a tide of northern victory from Georgia toward Virginia, Lee broke away from the trenches at Petersburg, where Grant had been besieging his army for nine months. Grant trapped him at Appomattox Court House (April 9, 1865), and the Confederacy flickered out.

On April 14, Abraham Lincoln was assassinated. The nation did not immediately realize its loss; indeed, only after another great war did we begin to take full measure of Lincoln's stature. He was one of the common people, sharing their tastes and foibles and sense of humor, yet gifted with the wisdom of a seer and the serenity of those touched by the spirit of God. Almost broken by the burden of a war he loathed, he lifted his people by precept and example to the supreme sacrifice. He was incapable of hatred, as of self-love. In his last days, he was preparing to wrestle with the foul passions that a costly victory creates, determined to obtain justice for the vanquished. . . . Yet how fortunate are we to have had our ideal and better selves made man so closely in our likeness that we may love him as a friend, and with such simplicity that his image may remain warm in our hearts from generation to generation.

If Lincoln's end was tragic, what shall we say of the consequences? For the manner of his taking off made irresistible a cry for vengeance that overwhelmed his wise and magnanimous policy. Not immediately, to be sure; for Vice-President Andrew Johnson, a Unionist from Tennessee, true-hearted as Lincoln but wanting his art in dealing with men, adopted Lincoln's policy of reconstruction. The blockade was promptly lifted; normal relations of trade and intercourse were established; and after the last Confederate army had surrendered in Texas, peace was officially proclaimed. Southerners who took the oath of allegiance were allowed to elect state legislatures, and send senators and representatives to Congress.

But when Congress convened in December 1865, it appeared that the balance of power was in the hands of the implacable die-hards of the Republican party—the Radicals, as they were then called. These men were Yankees from New England and the Middle West, who claimed a monopoly of righteousness. Throughout the war they had denounced Lincoln as a soft hitter and a man of words, little better than a southern sympathizer. Now they refused to seat the representatives of the reconstructed states; instead, they conducted an "investigation" which created the impression that southerners were inveterate rebels, awaiting the first opportunity to restore slavery and wreck the Union. Actually, as Grant and Sherman reported, the war-scarred South accepted defeat and emancipation without reserve, although her proud and self-respecting people would not confess sins of which they were unconscious, nor repudiate tried and proven leaders.

Military occupation of the South by federal troops led to many irritating incidents; and the new legislatures, composed for the most part of inexperienced men, did foolish things that gave color to the charge of inveteracy. Yet the Radical leaders, of whom Thaddeus Stevens was first, were actuated not so much by thirst for vengeance as by fear that the ex-slaves, for whom they felt responsible, would be kept down unless given the vote—and, less altruistically, by their anticipation that the Negro vote would extend the Republican party into the South. Northern idealists supported this Radical policy in the hope that the franchise would make the Negroes responsible citizens.

The reconstruction program went before the people in the congressional elections of 1866, which President Johnson lost by his crude oratory and the Radicals won by presenting the issue as one of loyalty against rebellion. Then the South was made to feel the rod. Johnson's reconstructed southern state governments were swept away. A new electorate of ex-slaves and poor whites, led by "carpetbaggers" from the North and supported by Union bayonets, set up legislatures which performed a grotesque parody of republican government. The Radicals' intention to guarantee political and economic liberty to the Negroes became fundamental law in the Fourteenth and Fifteenth Amendments to the Constitution (1868, 1870), although their provisions protecting the Negroes' new rights soon fell into desuetude.

Reconstruction created an intolerable situation for the

southern whites. Mulcted of their little property by the plundering taxes of the carpetbag legislatures, flouted and insulted by their former slaves, they retaliated with white terrorism. The Ku Klux Klan enforced labor contracts, "persuaded" many carpetbaggers to leave, and made it unhealthy for Negroes to be seen at polling places. In one state after another the Democratic party recovered control; by 1877 only South Carolina and Louisiana remained Republican. The first act of President Hayes, elected in 1876, was to remove the last federal garrisons from these states. Then they too fell under white and Democratic control.

This whole episode of Reconstruction was a signal proof that no government can long endure without the consent of the governed. Much harm was done. The "solid" Democratic South was formed; the colored people gained nothing by their premature power; and southern race relations were frozen in a pattern of conflict.

The Radicals, not content with imposing a congressional tyranny on the South, proposed to trample on the President and the Supreme Court. Their impeachment of Johnson on trumped-up and frivolous charges failed in the the Senate because some Republican senators cared more for justice than for party. General Grant obtained the Republican nomination in 1868 and served two terms as president. A leader ill-prepared for civil office, an honest man too tolerant of greedy friends, Grant made a sad administrative record. Yet he had the courage and wisdom to refer a question of national interest and honor—the *Alabama* claims—to international arbitration. To the end of his life, he remained modest, brave, and true.

While the South was struggling with a stark issue of race supremacy, the North strode forward to complete the conquest of the continent. New inventions turned ancient handicrafts into factory industries. Petroleum, discovered in

Pennsylvania just before the war, revolutionized rural lighting as coal gas had already done in the cities, and Thomas Edison began his practical applications of electricity. The Bessemer steel process was imported from England just when new and suitable ore beds were discovered near Lake Superior. The resulting cheap steel made possible a vast extension of railroad building and machinery, and the United States became the world's ironmaster.

Construction of the first transcontinental railroad link (between the Central Pacific and the Union Pacific) was pushed so rapidly from both ends that the lines were joined near Ogden, Utah, in 1869. A new wave of settlers, taking advantage of free farms under the Homestead Act of 1862, extended the corn belt into central Kansas and Nebraska and the wheat belt into northern Minnesota, where the Twin Cities, mere hamlets before the Civil War, became the world's center for milling flour. A thousand miles beyond, hard characters were roughing it and mining gold, silver, and lead in Missoula, Carson City, Cripple Creek, and a hundred other mining camps of the Rocky Mountains and the Sierra Nevada. Between the agricultural and the mining frontier, cattle and cowboy were pushing buffalo and Indian from the Great Plains and providing the big packers of Chicago and Kansas City with meat to be distributed world-wide in the newly invented refrigerator cars and ships.

Those who hoped that war would purge the nation of material corruptions and uplift the people through sacrifice were sadly disappointed. Profiteering, sudden prosperity, and cutthroat competition undermined the older business ethics and forced an alliance between business men and politicians. The latter were not slow to observe the power that lay in controlling the foreign-born vote and the profits to be made by granting favors to corporations and blackmailing honest business.

Business retaliated by controlling cities, and even states, with bought politicians. In New Hampshire as in California, no one could hope for a political career who was not the big railroad's vassal. "The stockholder has stepped into the place of the warlike baron," wrote Emerson in 1867. "The nobles shall not any longer, as feudal lords, have power of life and death over the churls, but now, in another shape, as capitalists, shall in all love and peace eat them up as before. Nay, government itself becomes the resort of those whom government was invented to restrain."

Yet all this was a mere foretaste of the development that was to come after 1877.

CHAPTER SIX

Power: 1877-1929

Politics had little influence on the general trend of American history during the generation after the Civil War. The Republican and Democratic parties became so equal in numbers and so fixed in composition that the turn of a doubtful state, or the slip of a candidate's tongue, might swing an election.

Reconstruction gave the Democrats the "solid South"; in the North tribal loyalty retained for them the increasing foreign-born vote and the dwindling number of native-borns who remembered Jackson. Republicans capitalized on the northern war spirit: whenever possible, it contested elections on old war issues and fought the Democrats as rebels and copperheads. Until 1904 every successful Republican presidential candidate was a veteran, most of them members of an "Ohio Dynasty" that seemed unshakeable.

There was no difference in principle between the two parties except on the tariff, and little difference in practice on that. They were simply two organized groups, one largely northern and the other largely southern, competing for place and power. Both parties neglected the army and allowed the navy to become fifth-rate; yet the United States won every diplomatic controversy with European powers.

In 1884, when the Republicans nominated the unsavory Blaine, the mugwumps (as the liberal wing was called) bolted and assisted Grover Cleveland. His was the first Democratic victory since 1856, though he was re-elected in 1892, largely because the cost of living shot up after the Republican tariff passed in President Harrison's administration. Cleveland had the obstinacy to insist on fulfilling campaign pledges and the bad luck to encounter hard times; the next Democratic victory came in 1912.

In the meantime, an economic and social evolution was creating a situation that would force a new issue into national policy: that of social justice. The decade after 1877 was the most ruthless period in the history of American business. Reckless competition and unchecked exploitation had brought a panic in 1873, as well as a series of violent and disastrous strikes. Business then reorganized its methods and goals by expanding mechanical improvements, mass production, employers' associations, combinations (of which railroads were the most powerful), and trusts (such as Standard Oil, the most lawless). Many citizens felt they had put down a slave power only to fall into the clutches of a more rapacious money power. A downward trend of prices after 1873 depressed the farmer, and his distress culminated in the lean 1890's.

Congress created the Interstate Commerce Commission in 1887 and passed the Sherman Antitrust Act of 1890; but the one had no teeth, and the other was based on a bad principle—that of "busting," rather than regulating, the big corporations, which were on the whole a natural and useful development in a capitalistic society. While European nations were bringing their corporations under control in order to protect the public, Americans remained reluctant to extend the power of government over industry. Big business kept alive old Jeffersonian prejudices while seeking Hamiltonian goals.

The colonial tradition that currency was the key to prosperity welled up again in one-idea parties such as the Greenbackers, who claimed that the gradual deflation of the paper dollar was enriching "bloated bondholders" at the expense of mere taxpayers. A more authentic note of hostility to privilege was sounded by the Populist party in 1890. What fun the eastern press had with the Populists' absurd proposals of postal savings banks, government ownership of railways, and the like—and with their leaders, "Sockless" Jerry Simpson and Mrs. Leake, who advised the farmers to raise less corn and more hell! But laughter changed to apprehension in 1892, when this party polled a million votes; and to something like terror in 1896, when the new wine of Populism, poured into the Democratic party, burst forth in the shape of William Jennings Bryan.

Mr. Bryan's cure-all for economic distress and financial tyranny was free silver. This new form of inflationist tradition meant that the United States Treasury should coin into dollars, each containing about fifty cents worth of bullion, all the silver that was offered by the mines. Cheap money would move the crops, pay off farm mortgages, and restore rural prosperity. The Democrats also demanded an income tax, a low tariff, and a considerable amount of state socialism.

Free silver, though not the sharpest issue, was the chief talking point of a frenzied contest. "Uncle" Mark Hanna shook down Wall Street for huge campaign contributions, while the silver miners came across generously for the "boy orator of the Platte," youngest and most eloquent of our presidential candidates. He carried a large part of the West; but money talked loudest in New York, and eastern wage-earners did not relish the idea of wages paid in depreciated dollars. "Uncle" Mark's protégé, William McKinley, won. Business could hardly have been more relieved if a Communist uprising had been suppressed.

The Republicans promptly raised the protective tariff to a new high level, and the return of prosperity seemed to confirm their principles and confound the prophets of disaster. But the problem of trusts and railroad regulation was beginning to worry even the easygoing McKinley, when Spain provided a diversion.

Cuba had been in something worse than its chronic state of revolution since 1895. American public opinion was already exercised over Spanish atrocities, when the battleship *Maine* blew up in Havana Harbor. Everyone assumed that the Spaniards had done it, and the howls of "Remember the *Maine*" and "Free Cuba" became irresistible. McKinley and his administration were pushed unwillingly into war, even though Spain was ready to grant Cuba autonomy or even independence.

The United States was unprepared and Spain even less so. Admiral Dewey sank one fleet in Manila Bay (May 1, 1898); Admiral Sampson ran another aground near Santiago; and "Teddy" Roosevelt, not quite "alone in Cuby" (as Mr. Dooley put it), swept aside the few Spanish troops who got in his way. Four months after the war was declared, Spain sued for peace; she wound up her long and glorious history in the New World by relinquishing Cuba and ceding Puerto Rico to the United States. Puerto Rico proved grateful for American rule, and Cuba was let out on a leash in 1903; but that leash, the Platt Amendment, was cut after thirty years.

By the same peace treaty, the United States purchased the Philippine Islands, which proved the most costly and complicated of our new responsibilities. Filipinos had been fighting for independence and supposed that the Americans had come to help. When McKinley decided it was our Christian duty to civilize the Philippine natives, they rebelled and kept up jungle warfare until 1901.

The Philippines gave us a stake in the Orient but turned our stomachs against further annexation of alien peoples. Economic penetration of Latin America had proved more profitable and less troublesome than the European form of imperialism. Occasionally Marines had to be landed to "preserve order," and in Haiti, at least, they made a somewhat prolonged stay; but these forcible occupations were finally liquidated under President Franklin Delano Roosevelt.

A new era opened with the new century, when the assassination of McKinley made his vice-president, Theodore Roosevelt, president of the United States. This youngest of our chief magistrates was admirably prepared by inheritance, training, and temperament. He understood the transformation that had come over the country in the past thirty years. He had positive ideas as to what to do about it, as well as the boundless vitality that is needed for a crusade against custom and privilege.

Undeterred by the Bryan wave of 1896, the trust movement developed. Denied the right to combine, competing businesses decided to unite. Tobacco, steel, oil, meat, and many other necessities of life were welded into supercorporations which strangled competition, placed labor at the mercy of capital, and, in many instances, mulcted the public by increased rates and prices to make dividends on swollen capitalization. Corruption of state legislatures and municipalities increased proportionately. Roosevelt's own class of moneyed easterners regarded this process as natural and proper, but discontent was increasing on the part of small businessmen, the salaried classes, and labor.

In many states, reformers, publicists, and a few politicians (such as La Follette of Wisconsin) were doing their best to restore standards of public virtue, obtain social legislation, and crush boss-ridden machines. These efforts, however, were unco-ordinated and were often rendered futile by courts which found them unconstitutional. Roosevelt, placing himself at the head of this great reform movement, accomplished the miracle of making the standpat Republican party an instrument of progress. He inaugurated what we may call the "progressive era" (1901-17), when the structure and processes of government, state and federal, were adapted to the economic and social changes that had transformed the life and business of almost the entire country.

Roosevelt's first efforts were a much-needed housecleaning of the federal administration from the waste, corruption, and inefficiency that had accumulated under the "Ohio Dynasty." He extended the civil service rules over numerous classes of federal employees and infused some of his own vigor into the public offices. His love for the great outdoors and his desire to husband national resources led him to curb the waste and looting of government land, to create forest reserves, and to establish new national parks. He used the government's prosecuting power under the Sherman Antitrust Act to check some of the worst abuses of monopoly. Congress, at his recommendation, protected the consumer from fraud and adulteration by passing the Pure Food and Drug Act of 1906. The Hepburn Act of that year gave the Interstate Commerce Commission at least its milk teeth.

By preaching civic righteousness and practicing public virtue, Theodore Roosevelt did more to educate the American people in the principles of good government and unselfish service than all the textbooks on civics ever written.

After the Spanish-American War, Europeans expected America to take a leading place in world politics, and Roosevelt did not disappoint them. In his hands, the Monroe Doctrine became something more than a warning against intervention: it became an assumption of responsibility for the weaker Caribbean republics. In the Far East, Roosevelt and Secretary of State John Hay exerted themselves to preserve the territorial integrity of China; and the President's secret diplomacy helped bring the Russo-Japanese War to a close. With the British government he reached a complete understanding on all points of friction, and the new international Hague Tribunal received from him its first two cases. "Walk softly, and carry a big stick" was Roosevelt's policy. The "big stick" fell heavily on Panama, the weakest portion of Colombia's anatomy, but it was used elsewhere for peace and justice.

In deference to tradition, Roosevelt declined in 1908 the third term that the nation was eager to bestow; he nominated a friend, William Howard Taft, as his successor and sailed away to hunt big game in Africa. But Taft lacked the ability and temperament to continue the Roosevelt policies. Much useful and progressive legislation was passed during his term, but perhaps more was thwarted by an unreformed Senate and a House under the iron hand of the speaker, "Uncle Joe" Cannon.

Roosevelt returned from Africa in 1910 to find his party split into "insurgents," who were trying to develop a progressive program, and "regulars," who considered that reform had gone far enough. The fall elections were a Democratic landslide, for the cost of living was rapidly increasing, and the inordinately high Paine-Aldrich tariff of 1909, which Taft had mistakenly approved, convinced the country that he had sold out to the "interests."

As the election of 1912 approached, Roosevelt was frequently urged to come out for the Republican nomination against Taft. He repeatedly refused, but the crown was offered once too often; he finally agreed. When the Republican convention "steam-rollered" him out of the nomination which he felt to be his due, he bolted and formed the Progressive party.

But his hope of breaking the old, meaningless party lines with the massed forces of progress was thwarted by the Democrats. With unexpected wisdom they nominated their rising progressive, Woodrow Wilson, formerly president of

Princeton University, now governor of New Jersey. Wilson won the election. Taft fell below Roosevelt in the popular vote, carrying only Utah and Vermont, but those who predicted that the GOP had gone the way of the Federalists and Whigs were premature.

Roosevelt's technique had been a forced feeding of his reluctant party, but the suave bedside manner of Dr. Wilson induced his Democratic patient to take the same progressive diet without protest. It was marvelous how that former professor led a party of negative and states' rights tradition into an enlightened and constructive nationalism. Wilson's strength lay in his character and intellect. Lacking the robust good-fellowship which gave "Teddy" more personal friends than any man in the country, or the common touch that helped Lincoln, he yet had Jefferson's power to express popular aspirations. His serene, almost pontifical self-confidence was profoundly irritating to "red-blooded" and "two-fisted" men, many of whom disliked his policy and refused to admit his sincerity.

The Democratic party promptly redeemed its pledge of tariff reduction in the Underwood Act of 1913, lowest since the Civil War. The income tax amendment (No. 16) to the Constitution, sponsored by Roosevelt, was ratified in 1913. The trust problem was dealt with in the Clayton Antitrust Act—"labor's charter of freedom," as labor leader Samuel Gompers called it for the anti-injunction clause.

The Federal Reserve Act of 1913 superseded an outworn national banking system and sought to provide machinery to flatten out the peaks and valleys of prosperity and depression. Wilson also endeavored to allay Latin America's growing apprehension of us, and refused to take advantage of the weakness and distraction of Mexico.

Before the Democratic program had been fairly developed, war burst upon the world. Wilson issued a formal declaration of neutrality and asked his countrymen to be neutral in word and thought, but that was impossible. The isolationist tradition of American foreign policy, carefully built up since the days of Monroe, was shattered by our strong cultural and racial relations with Europe. Violent partisanship succeeded the first feelings of horror and repulsion. Pro-Germanism was confined largely to certain German-Americans, whose sentiment for the fatherland had been carefully fostered by the German government and who felt their own dignity and consequence heightened by the colossal successes of the German army. They found ready support from certain Irish-Americans, who had cherished ancient animosities. Pro-Allied feeling was at first confined largely to the well-to-do on both coasts, who by education, travel, or personal relations had sympathy and affection for England and France. Thousands of their young men enlisted in the Canadian army, the Foreign Legion, and the American ambulance service in France. Gradually pro-Allied sentiment extended inland and broadened. The average American had no means, even when he had the desire, to probe the real causes of the war, but the ruthless methods of the Germans were repulsive to his taste, whilst the heroic resistance of France and the quiet determination of England compelled his admiration. He began to wonder what his own fate would be if Germany conquered Europe.

American industry, after adjusting itself to war conditions, began to supply enormous quantities of arms and munitions, food and manufactures, to the Allies, who commanded the sea. The Allied governments, however, in their zeal to isolate Germany, controlled neutral trade and shipping in a manner that revived memories of 1812. The President's notes on the subject were much resented by the Allies, and his failure to do more than send notes angered Germany.

Allied sea power, though disturbing to old trade routes, gave Americans new business; but there could be no compensation for the American lives taken by German submarines. The sinking of the *Lusitania* (May 7, 1915) brought the war closer and crystallized public opinion into two groups —those who demanded immediate preparedness for war against Germany, and those who believed in neutrality at all costs. The noisy advocacy of neutrality by pro-Germans and socialists tended to discredit it and to weaken the influence of the President, who was quietly working through Colonel House to bring about peace. His efforts failed, since the Allied governments dared not consent to a peace treaty while Germany occupied their territory, and Germany wanted still more territory.

Wilson's stiff notes to Germany after the *Lusitania* affair caused the resignation of Secretary of State Bryan, who believed that the loss of American lives on a belligerent's ship was not a matter of national honor. The same view, pressed by Republicans in Congress, very nearly resulted in a joint resolution warning American travelers to stay at home. In August 1915 the German government pledged itself to sink no more passenger ships without warning, but the President came out in favor of military and naval preparedness.

So matters stood in the middle of 1916, when Wilson came up for re-election. His social legislation was thoroughly disliked by big business; his Mexican policy seemed indecisive; his neutrality was regarded as pusillanimous by pro-Allies and criminally partisan by pro-Germans. The Republicans nominated Supreme Court Justice Charles Evans Hughes, who had not offended anyone, and Roosevelt supported him. But Wilson had won a large part of the Progressive vote, and Hughes's dull campaign lost him votes where-ever he went. The slogan that Wilson "kept us out of war" appealed to the common people, and they re-elected him to the presidency.

Woodrow Wilson, as he admitted, had a "one-track mind," and the track was peace. Only after the failure of his last effort at mediation, in January 1917, did he begin to feel that America could best help the world by taking a decided part with the Allies. Everything then began to break that way. Germany announced unrestricted submarine warfare on January 31 and torpedoed eight American vessels in February and March. An intercepted note to Mexico, promising to help her recover Texas and Arizona, was a stunning blow to the pro-Germans. The overthrow of the Tsar in March seemed to remove the last taint of autocracy from the Allied cause.

On April 2, as soon as the new Congress convened, Wilson appeared before it in joint session to ask for a declaration of war against Germany. "It is a fearful thing," he concluded, "to lead this great peaceful people into war, into the most terrible and disastrous of all wars, civilization itself seeming to be in the balance. But the right is more precious than peace, and we shall fight for the things which we have always carried nearest our hearts—for democracy, for the right of those who submit to authority to have a voice in their own governments, for the rights and liberties of small nations, for a universal dominion of right by such a concert of free peoples as shall bring peace and safety to all nations and make the world itself at last free. To such a task we can dedicate our lives and our fortunes, everything that we are and everything that we have, with the pride of those who know that the day has come when America is privileged to spend her blood and her might for the principles that gave her birth and happiness and the peace which she has treasured. God helping her, she can do no other."

In the small hours of Good Friday morning, April 6, 1917, Congress formally declared a war whose effects will be felt for generations. One of its consequences was the Bolshevik revolution in Russia.

As a war leader, Wilson rose almost to the stature of Lincoln, though without attaining his breadth. He stirred men to high endeavor with words and phrases that sang in their hearts. The high objects for which he accepted war lifted the great conflict to something like a crusade for world peace and eternal justice. As commander in chief, he gave his confidence to General Pershing, who deserved it. But as a political strategist the President was woefully inept. He ignored the secret treaties which made his sort of peace impossible and threw American resources into Europe with no guarantee that they would effect his goals.

Wilson must also share the responsibility for deflecting the American purpose from his own high aims to mere victory: from loving justice to hating "Huns." The Allied governments pleaded haste lest they perish; the German submarine warfare redoubled its intensity; and the October revolution in Russia removed that great country from the Allied side. Under these pressures the President became absorbed in the idea of "force without stint." He allowed those directing his propaganda service to appeal to the basest passions, even to discourage talk about the League of Nations. The public, stirred to a 'frenzy by the thought of enemy agents in its midst, supported the authorities in an inquisition of public opinion then unprecedented in American history. To uphold Wilson's own high ideals appeared, in some quarters, to be sedition.

Yet no one who lived through those fateful months of 1917 and 1918 can forget the exultation that came from taking part in a mighty enterprise. Americans gave freely of their money, their services, and their lives. The draft went through without a hitch, and millions of Americans were transported to France with less fuss and friction than thousands had been sent to Cuba in 1898. Profiteering, encouraged by the cost-plus system of government contracts, flourished as in every war. But artists designed war posters; composers wrote patriotic songs; advertisers "sold" the war to the people; classes and communities vied with one another in oversubscribing their quotas to the several liberty loans and to the various drives for the Red Cross, the YMCA, the Knights of Columbus, and other auxiliary services. Even the radical lumberjacks, the "wobblies," of the Far West were induced to get out airplane spruce for a "capitalist war." Mr. Hoover's conservation program went through largely by voluntary co-operation, and a nation of heavy eaters submitted to wheatless and meatless days in order to share its plenty with the war workers of Europe.

The German drive on the western front in the spring of 1918 accelerated our war effort. Every available ton of shipping was commandeered to get men across. In July came news that Americans had helped to stop the German drive in Château-Thierry, and as more American divisions relieved the weary French on the western front, the great offensive began through the Forest of Argonne to the Meuse. In September the Central Powers—Germany and her allies—began to crack. First Bulgaria threw in the sponge; then Turkey; then Austria; and in October came an astounding peace overture from the new German chancellor. The President replied that he could not deal with the Imperial Government. At his word, the Hohenzollern monarchy crumbled, and the Kaiser fled to Holland. Superpatriots were looking forward to a glorious march on Berlin when, on November 11, 1918, the new German republic accepted the terms of armistice.

The President himself was largely to blame for not obtaining his dearest wish as a war object, the adhesion of his country to a strong League of Nations. He made several political misplays. In October 1918 he appealed to the people to elect Democrats in the fall elections. They resented the suggestion that his party had a monopoly of patriotism, and disobeyed. From a sense of duty, but without thinking out the consequences, Wilson decided to attend the Peace Conference in person, thus losing his power as an embodied voice expressing the aspirations of mankind. He failed to associate with him in the peace commission any prominent Republican.

Whether it would have been better for the United States to have accepted the Treaty of Versailles and the League of Nations is a question on which honest men may differ to the end of time. But the treaty was opposed in the United States more for its virtues than for its defects. Most of the Republicans would have underwritten the "strong peace" that Georges Clemenceau wanted, but the League of Nations they considered an "entangling alliance." Theodore Roosevelt and Senator Lodge had personal scores to settle with Wilson, and the other Republican leaders were determined to prevent the Democratic party from capitalizing on the World War, as their own party had on the Civil War. They found ready supporters in the veterans, who brought home no love of late comrades in arms, and among various racial groups: Italian-Americans who blamed Wilson for the loss of Fiume, German-Americans who wanted revenge, Irish-Americans who viewed the League as a British trap. Many liberals who had followed Wilson in war for the high ends he sought regarded the treaty as much too harsh on Germany, and the League as a device to impose an unjust peace.

The treaty would have been ratified in some shape if the President had been willing to accept the Lodge reservations, but he refused to compromise in Washington as he had in

Paris. When he made this decision (November 18, 1919), he was already suffering from a paralytic stroke; on resuming his seat at the cabinet table in April 1920, he was a mere shadow of his former self. Yet the country had changed more than he. When the war ended, America had not yet reached the peak of effort that the European nations had long since passed. The armistice left a sense of frustration among many war enthusiasts, whose fighting spirit was now transferred to supposed domestic enemies.

Socialism and communism were generally regarded in the United States as crank notions of the foreign-born until 1917, when they assumed a portentous shape in Russia. Actually the Third International destroyed the American Socialist party, leaving a mere handful of ardent Communists who could hardly affect a nation where the working people enjoyed a high standard of living; but many patriotic organizations and individuals, left without other occupation in 1919, made it their business to prove the contrary. A. Mitchell Palmer, attorney general and presidential aspirant, inaugurated a series of "red raids"—an orgy of lawless violence by officers of the law, in which aliens and citizens were arrested and imprisoned without warrant, men were torn from their families and deported, the free expression of opinion was suppressed, and the constitutional guarantees of personal liberty that the American Revolution had consecrated were torn to shreds.

A new Ku Klux Klan, formed to capitalize on hatred of Catholic and Jew, Negro and foreigner, spread into every state of the Union. Veterans' associations lobbied for repressive legislation. The fundamentalist movement in the Protestant churches began its drive on modern science. And all these organizations had much success in making public schools the vehicle of their mistaken patriotism. It was a time when everyone you met had private knowledge of some astounding conspiracy to undermine the home, the church, or the Constitution. Pacifists were alleged to be in collusion with Communists to extend the rule of Russia; Rhodes scholars were to induct the United States back into the British Empire; Catholics were hiding firearms under their churches; and international Jewish bankers were trying to enslave us all. Government by law almost abdicated in favor of government by snooping.

The country as a whole turned to material pursuits. A debauch of spending followed the war, as the millions of people who had attained wages of higher purchasing power squandered the increase on luxury. Violence became no less common merely because it ceased to be taught as the soldier's duty, and the army discipline—of which much had been hoped—was dissipated by peace. The prohibition amendment (No. 18) floated in on the tide of war enthusiasm, and the Volstead Act, which provided for its enforcement, went into effect at this moment when the ancient ties of law and custom were relaxed.

Under these circumstances the Republicans, by promising prosperity and isolation, easily won in 1920. The new president, Warren G. Harding, resembled the kindly and easygoing McKinley; his election meant a restoration of the Ohio Dynasty and a return to the political practices of the Mark Hanna era. His friends followed him to Washington and proceeded to extract graft from the shipping board, the liquidation of war contracts, the veterans' bureau, sequestered German property, and government oil lands. Although many of these thefts and frauds were exposed and two members of the President's cabinet were shown to be involved, public opinion was singularly tolerant.

President Harding considered American participation in the League of Nations a closed question; but former Justice Hughes, his able secretary of state, sent delegates to several of the League commissions and advanced the reparations question to a just, if not a satisfactory, conclusion. His supposedly great achievement was the disarmament conference with Japan in Washington (1921) and the series of naval disarmament treaties which established the 5-5-3 ratio for capital ships of the United States, Great Britain, and Japan. This, as a device to preserve the peace, proved worse than useless.

Fear of an inundation of pauper labor from Europe and of racial stocks that would supposedly hinder the Americanization process produced a radical change in American immigration policy. The act of 1924 (amending that of 1921) restricted annual immigration—which had exceeded 1,200,000 in three separate years before the war—to 165,000, apportioned among the several nations on the basis of their representation in the United States in 1890. This heavily reduced immigration from eastern and southern Europe.

President Harding died in office on August 2, 1923. He was succeeded by the vice-president, Calvin Coolidge of Massachusetts. Shrewd, smug, and cautious, Coolidge restored order to the demoralized administration, won golden opinions from the average small-town American, kept his party united, and obtained its nomination in 1924. Among the western farmers, who suffered keenly from postwar deflation, there was discontent; but no Jackson or Bryan came forth. The Farmer-Labor party, a hopeless combination, nominated Senator La Follette, who carried only his home state. A long-drawnout contest for the presidential nomination between W. G. McAdoo, Wilson's former secretary of the treasury, and Governor "Al" Smith of the Sidewalks of New York, almost split the Democratic party. "Cal" Coolidge was overwhelmingly elected president. Yet little more than half the voters took the trouble to cast their ballots.

President Coolidge and the Congress fulfilled their

mandate to maintain the tariff, push our foreign trade, reduce taxes, and avoid unsettling legislation. He was troubled by the increasing difficulty of enforcing the prohibition amendment and by chronic unrest in the wheat belt; but from the press he received support, even adulation, such as none of his predecessors had enjoyed. In foreign affairs, apart from a Marine expeditionary force to Nicaragua, Coolidge worked for peace. The appointment of his friend Dwight W. Morrow as ambassador to Mexico brought an instant change for the better in relations with our touchy and suspicious neighbor. Senator Borah's program for the "outlawry of war" reached partial fruition in the Kellogg-Briand Pact of July 1928, in which fifteen nations, formally renouncing war as a national policy, pledged themselves to arbitrate all their disputes. This proved to be another delusion: no nation took it seriously.

In the presidential campaign of 1928, the personality of the losing candidate, Alfred E. Smith, a successful governor of New York but little known outside that state, succeeded in arousing popular interest in politics as no one since Roosevelt had done. He asked for election on the ground of the failure of prohibition, the corrupt record of the Harding administration, the failure of the Republican party to do anything for farm relief, and the growing insolence and tightening grip of the electric-light and power interests. He was handicapped by his Catholic religion, his "wet" record, and his earlier Tammany affiliations.

Herbert Hoover, without the magnetic personality of his opponent, was widely known for his work as food administrator during the war, as organizer of relief to Europe on an unprecedented scale, and as secretary of commerce under Harding and Coolidge. His campaign was largely a promise to continue the prosperity of the Coolidge era and an appeal for stability. Hoover carried southern states which had voted

Democratic since Reconstruction days, as well as the entire West and all the northern states but two. Smith's popular vote fell far behind, and Hoover won a sweeping victory in the electoral college.

In 1929 the stock market crashed, and the extended depression that followed—which President Hoover and the Republicans seemed helpless to cope with—brought about in 1932 the election of Franklin D. Roosevelt and his "New Deal."

In 1933, Adolf Hitler seized brutal control of the German government, and his expansionist policies led to the Second World War, into which the United States was precipitated by the Japanese attack on Pearl Harbor (December 7, 1941). That war and its results forced upon the United States a world leadership which she had not sought and for which she was not prepared.

Even before these events, the United States had evolved from a country of political experiment—a debtor to Europe and a radical disturber of established government—into a wealthy and conservative country, the world's banker and stabilizer, the most powerful enemy to violent revolution. American residence, once the right of the "poorest child of Adam's kin," had become a jealously guarded privilege. Americans had obtained a degree of comfort and social security beyond the dreams of departed philanthropists—and their standard of living has continued to rise.

In the process some of our old rugged virtues have been lost, but much of the old neighborliness and concern for social welfare have lasted—and, indeed, have been extended to include not only North America and Europe, but also Latin America and the new nations of Asia and Africa.

Before us lies the future, full of questions for a country still young as nations go, though prematurely old in experience. Whither lies our destiny? To maintain the vast and complicated edifice of the western alliance against Communism is a strain on the thought and life of the nation. The development of nuclear fission and its application to weapons means a touchy balance between self-defense and total destruction—a dilemma which has almost completely transformed the basic assumptions of foreign and military policy.

The dominant and pervasive issue of our time, not only here but the world over, is man's effort to control the forces of destruction which his ingenuity has brought into play.

The central paradox is that, in the second half of the twentieth century, our future on this continent is as insecure as it was in the sixteenth century, when our first European ancestors were faced with the daily hazards of nature and the Indians.

We trust that our courage and character may be as successful in this crisis as they were in those early days; that a pattern of peaceful coexistence with Communism may be found as Christianity once had to find it with Islam.

Above all, we hope that forces now latent or unseen may quicken the nation to new life and direct her mighty energy to some spiritual achievement that will shine down the ages, as the glory of ancient Greece still shines for us.

Index

Abolitionist movement, 40
Adams, John, 18, 28; elected President, 30
Adams, John Quincy, becomes President, 35
Adams, Samuel, 19, 20
Alabama, secedes, 51
Alabama claims, 59
Albany (N.Y.), 14
Amazon, conquest of, 4
America, discovery of, 3; producer of raw materials, 5-6
American Indians, 1, 3, 5
American Revolution, causes of, 17-19; fighting in, 19; a social revolution, 20; reasons for victory, 21-22
Antietam, Battle of, 54
Antigua, 6
Appomattox, battle of, 56
Aristocracy, and American revolution, 20
Arkansas, joins Confederacy, 52
Articles of Confederation, 23
Aztecs, 2

Balboa, explorer, 4
Baltimore, Lord, 9
Bank of the United States, 27, 35, 42
Barbados, 6
Bermuda, 6
Bessemer steel process, 60
Bill of Rights, 23
Blaine, James G., 62
Borah, Senator William E., 79
Boston, settled, 10; and religious growth, 13
Boston Tea Party, 19
Bradford, Governor William, 10

Brown, John, 49-50
Bryan, William Jennings, 64
Buchanan, James, 44; becomes President, 49
Bull Run, battles at, 54
Burr, Aaron, 28

Cabot, John, 3
Cabral, Pedro, 4
Calhoun, John C., 32, 35; nationalism of, 42-43; on slavery, 47
California, gold discovered in, 47; acquisition of, 48
Calvert, George. *See* Lord Baltimore
Calvinism, 11
Canada, and War of 1812, 32-33
Cannon, Joseph, Speaker of the House, 68
Carpetbaggers, 58
Cartier, Jacques, 4
Central America, Spanish exploration, 4
Champlain, Samuel, discovers Quebec, 4
Charles I, 11; and New England colonies, 13-14
Charles II, and New Netherland, 14
Charleston, 15
Chattanooga, battle at, 55
Christianity, Indians converted to, 5
Church of England, effect of, 9, 10
Civil War, 52-57; forces causing, 36-42; tension before outbreak, 50-52; European intervention, 54; battles, 54-56; end of, 56; moral effect, 60
Civilization, early, 1-3
Clay, Henry, 32, 35; and nullifica-

82